R U S H

RECORDED VERSIONS GUITAR

AUTHENTIC TRANSCRIPTIONS
WITH NOTES AND TABLATURE

The Spirit of Radio: Greate... 87

Music transcriptions by Jordan Baker, Adonai Booth, Jeff Jacobson, Paul Pappas and Ron Piccione

ISBN 978-1-5400-7194-1

HAL•LEONARD®

Visit Hal Leonard Online at
www.halleonard.com

Contact us:
Hal Leonard
7777 West Bluemound Road
Milwaukee, WI 53213
Email: info@halleonard.com

In Europe, contact:
Hal Leonard Europe Limited
42 Wigmore Street
Marylebone, London, W1U 2RN
Email: info@halleonardeurope.com

In Australia, contact:
Hal Leonard Australia Pty. Ltd.
4 Lentara Court
Cheltenham, Victoria, 3192 Australia
Email: info@halleonard.com.au

4	Working Man
22	Fly by Night
28	2112 – I Overture/II Temples of Syrinx
39	Closer to the Heart
50	The Trees
59	Spirit of Radio
70	Freewill
79	Limelight
89	Tom Sawyer
97	Red Barchetta
110	New World Man
115	Subdivisions
127	Distant Early Warning
137	The Big Money
148	Force Ten
163	Time Stand Still
173	GUITAR NOTATION LEGEND

Working Man

Words and Music by Alex Lifeson and Geddy Lee

*Composite arrangement

**Chord symbols reflect implied harmony.

1. Well,

(3.) I get up at sev-en, yeah,__ and I go to work__ at__ nine.__

I got no time for liv-in'. Yes, I'm work-in' all__ the__ time. It

seems to me__ I can live my__ life__ a lot bet-ter than I think I am.

Guitar Solo
Slightly faster ♩ = 156

E5

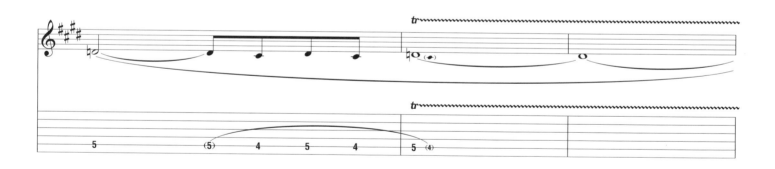

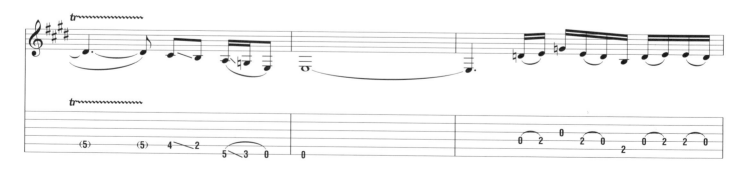

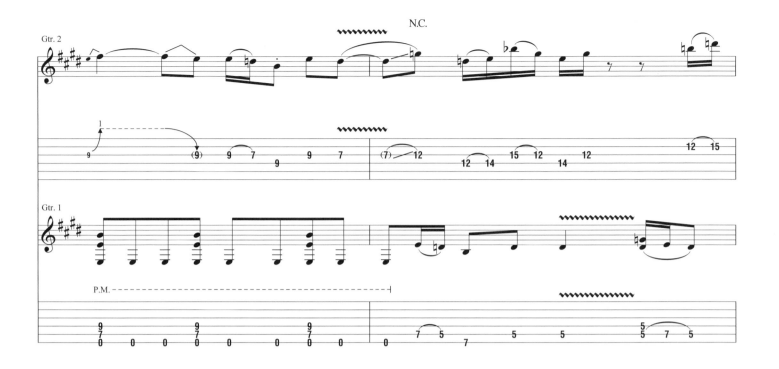

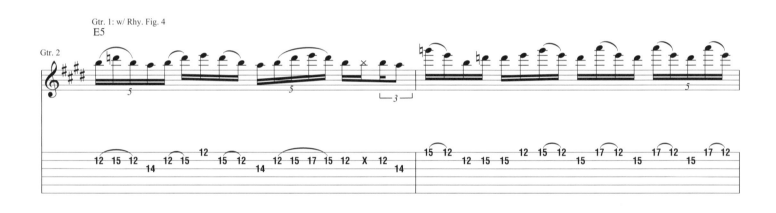

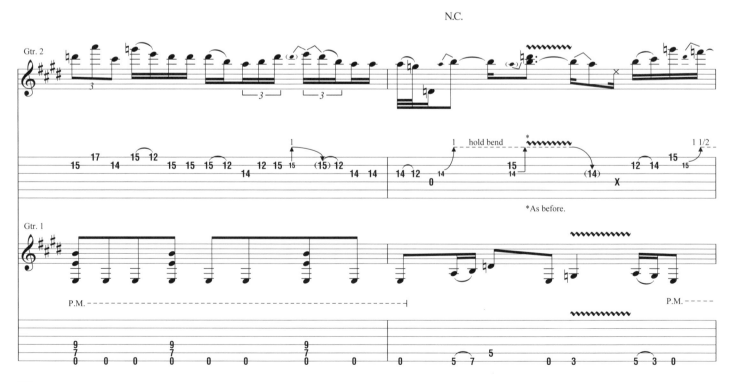

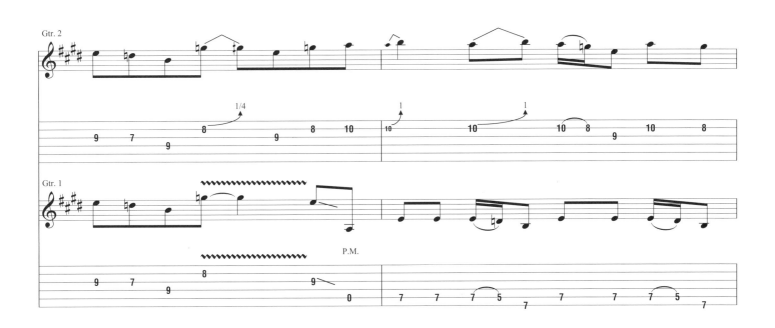

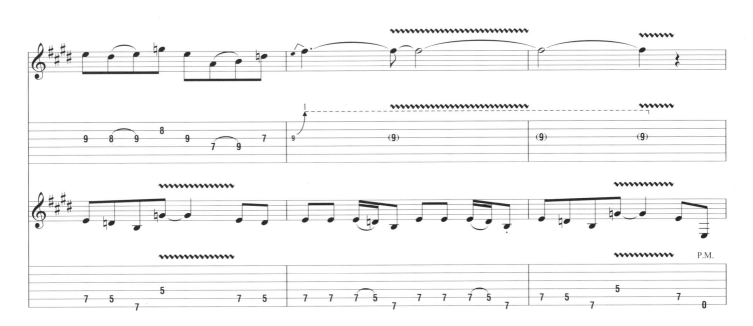

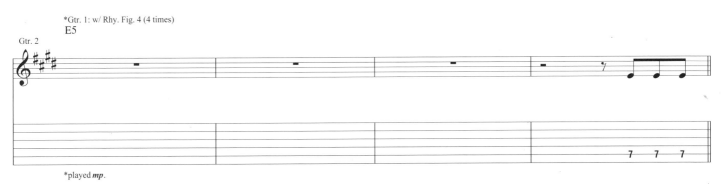

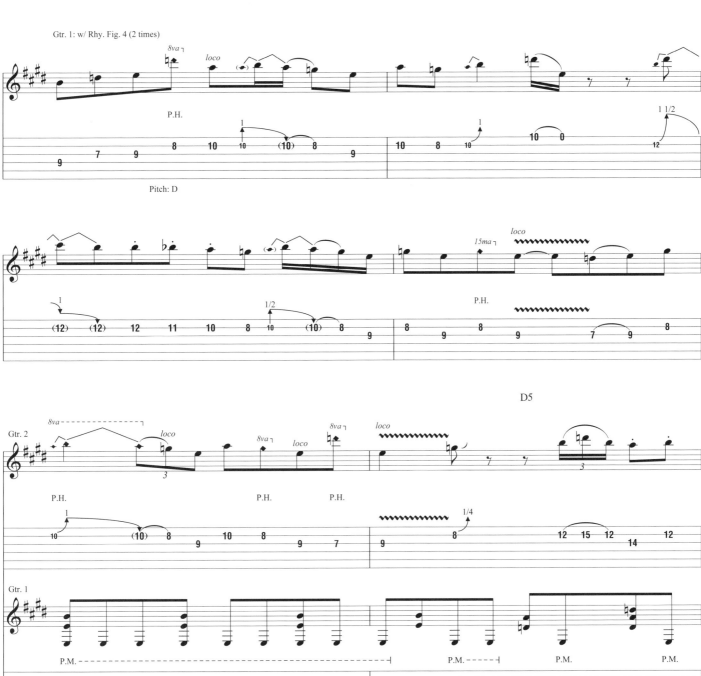

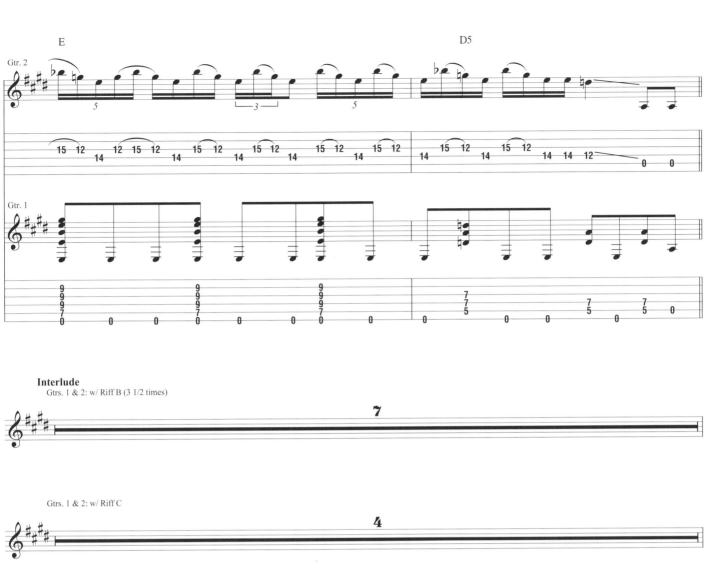

Interlude
Gtrs. 1 & 2: w/ Riff B (3 1/2 times)

Gtrs. 1 & 2: w/ Riff C

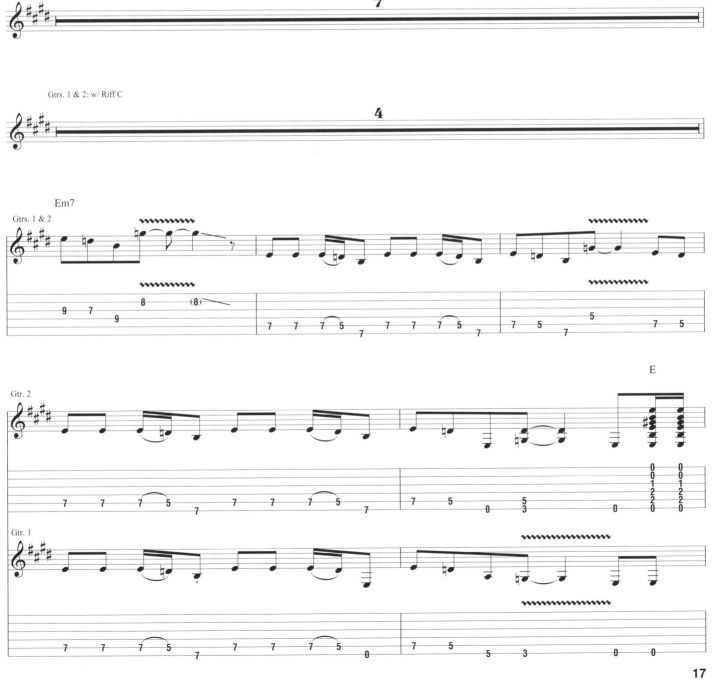

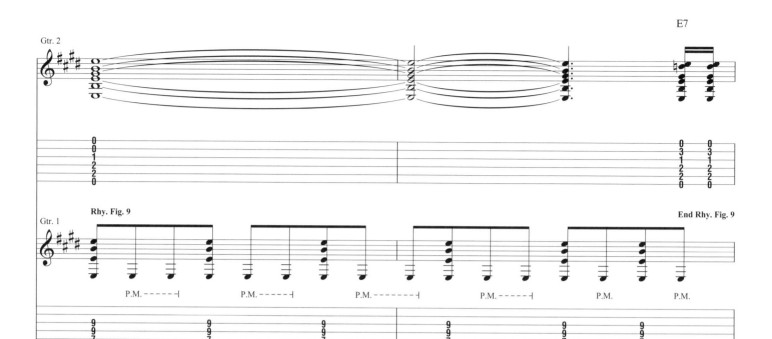

Gtr. 1: w/ Rhy. Fig. 9 (1 1/2 times)

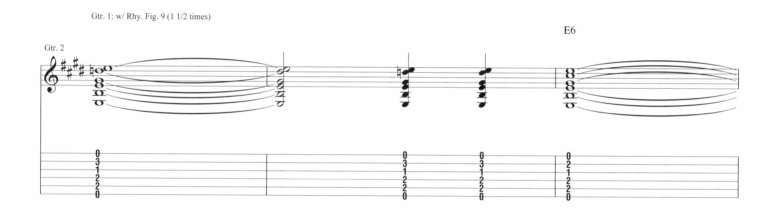

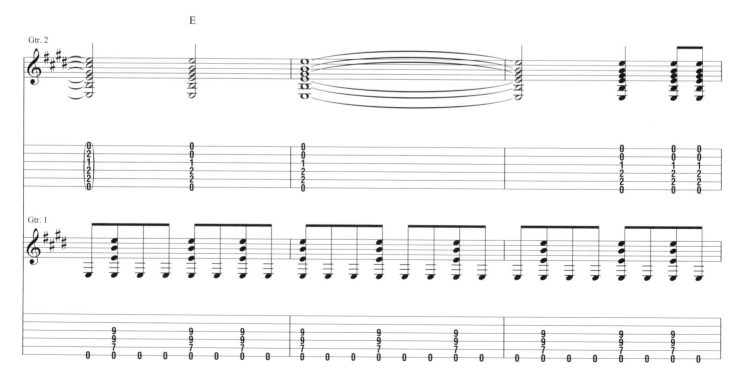

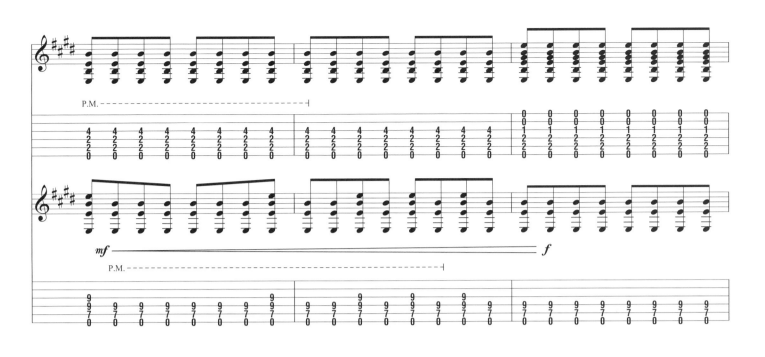

Slower ♩ = 80

D.S. al Coda

Gtr. 1: w/ Rhy. Fig. 2

E5　　　　　　　D5　　A5　　　　E　　　　　C5　　D5

3. Well,

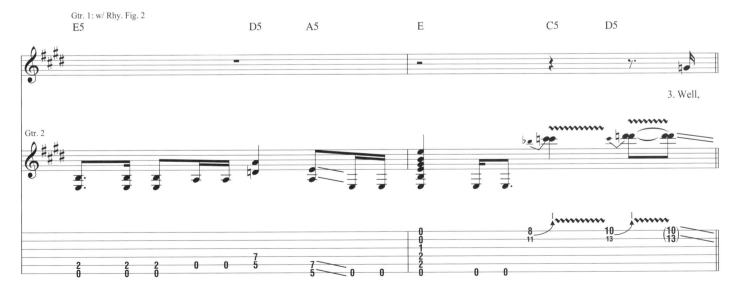

Coda

Gtrs. 1 & 2: w/ Rhy. Fig. 2 (1st 2 meas., 2 times)

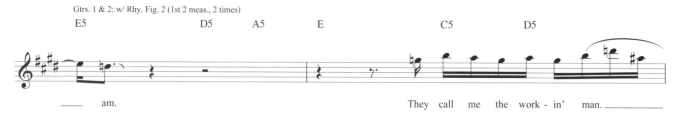

___ am.   They call me the work - in' man. ___

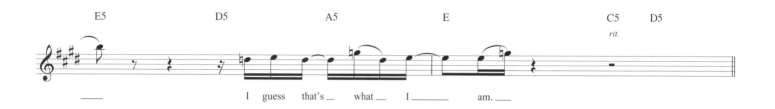

___   I guess that's __ what __ I ____ am. ___

Outro

Gtrs. 1 & 2

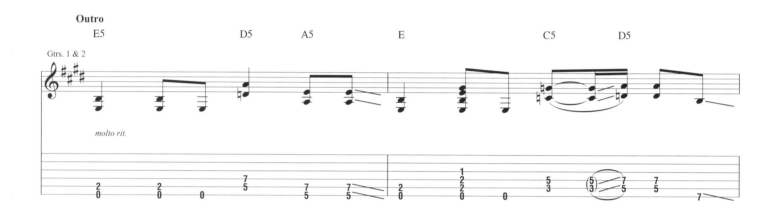

molto rit.

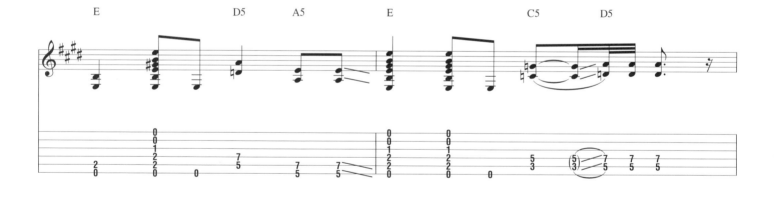

Free time

N.C.

Play 9 times

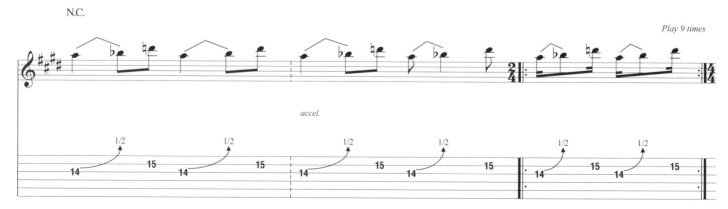

accel.

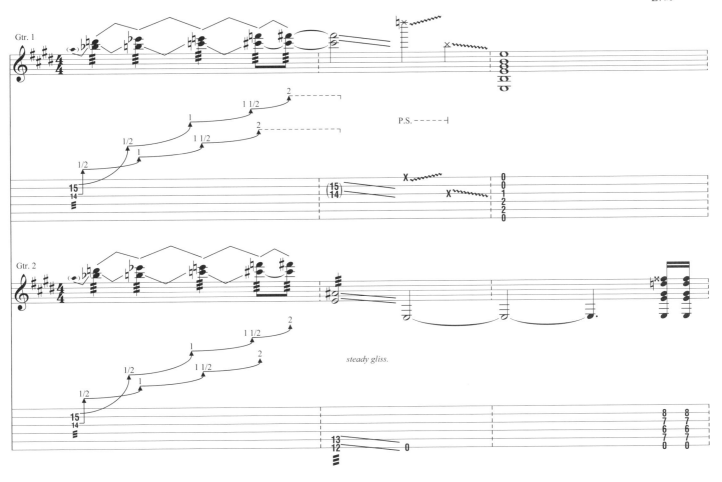

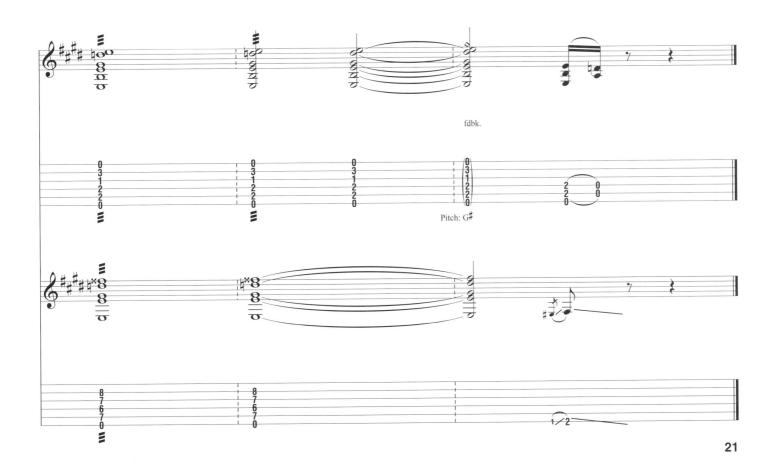

Fly by Night

Words and Music by Geddy Lee and Neil Peart

Copyright © 1975 Anthem Core Music Publishing
Copyright Renewed
All Rights Administered by Anthem Entertainment LP
All Rights Reserved   Used by Permission

22

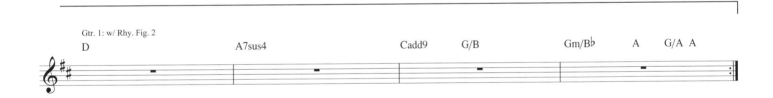

Guitar Solo

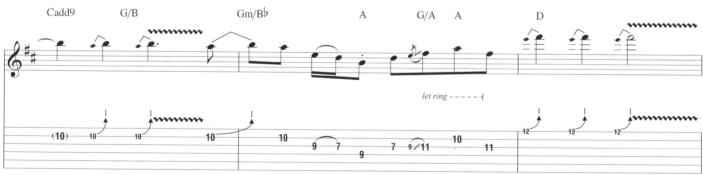

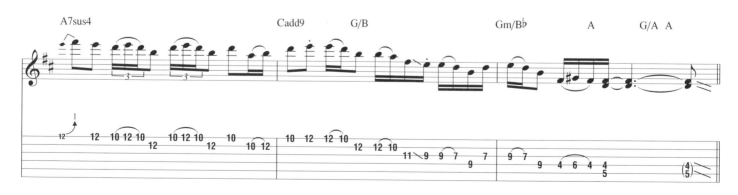

Chorus

Fly by night a-way from here, change my life a-gain.

Fly by night, good-bye, my dear. My ship is-n't com-ing and I just can't pre-tend.

Bridge

Start a new chap-ter, I find what I'm af-ter, it's chang-ing ev-'ry day.

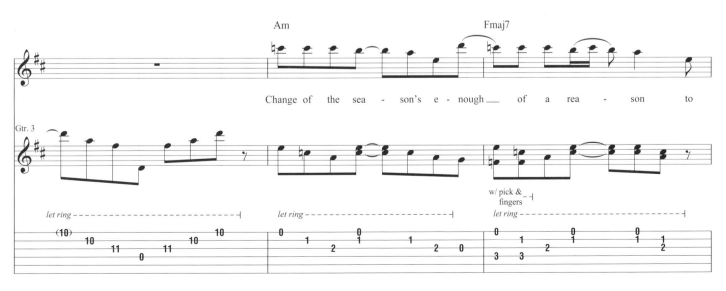

Change of the sea-son's e-nough of a rea-son to

want to get ___ a - way. Qui - et and pen - sive, ___ my

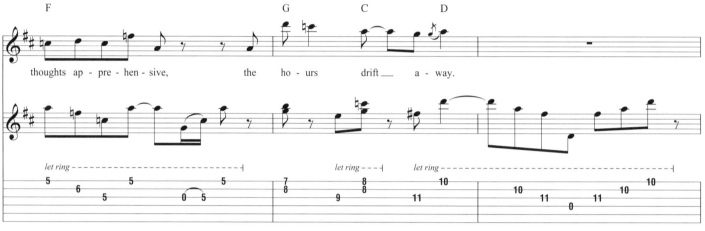

thoughts ap - pre - hen - sive, the ho - urs drift ___ a - way.

Leav - ing my home - land, play - ing a lone ___ hand, my life be - gins ___ to - day.

Outro-Chorus

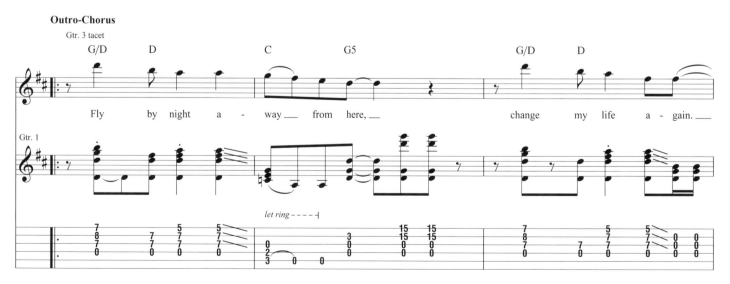

Fly by night a - way ___ from here, ___ change my life a - gain. ___

2112
I. Overture

Words and Music by Alex Lifeson, Geddy Lee and Neil Peart

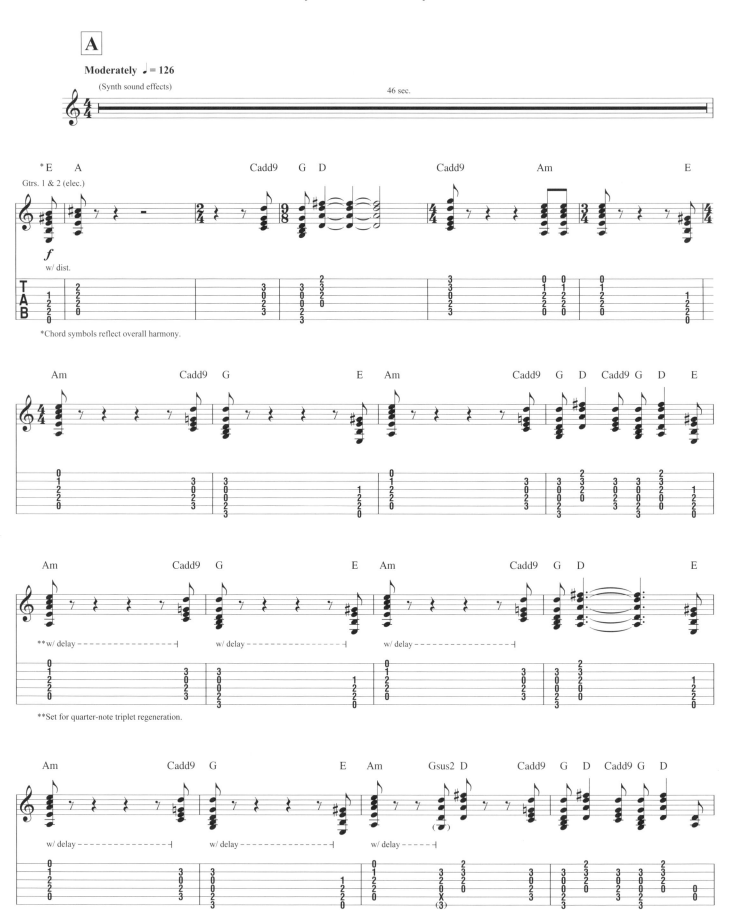

*Chord symbols reflect overall harmony.

**w/ delay

**Set for quarter-note triplet regeneration.

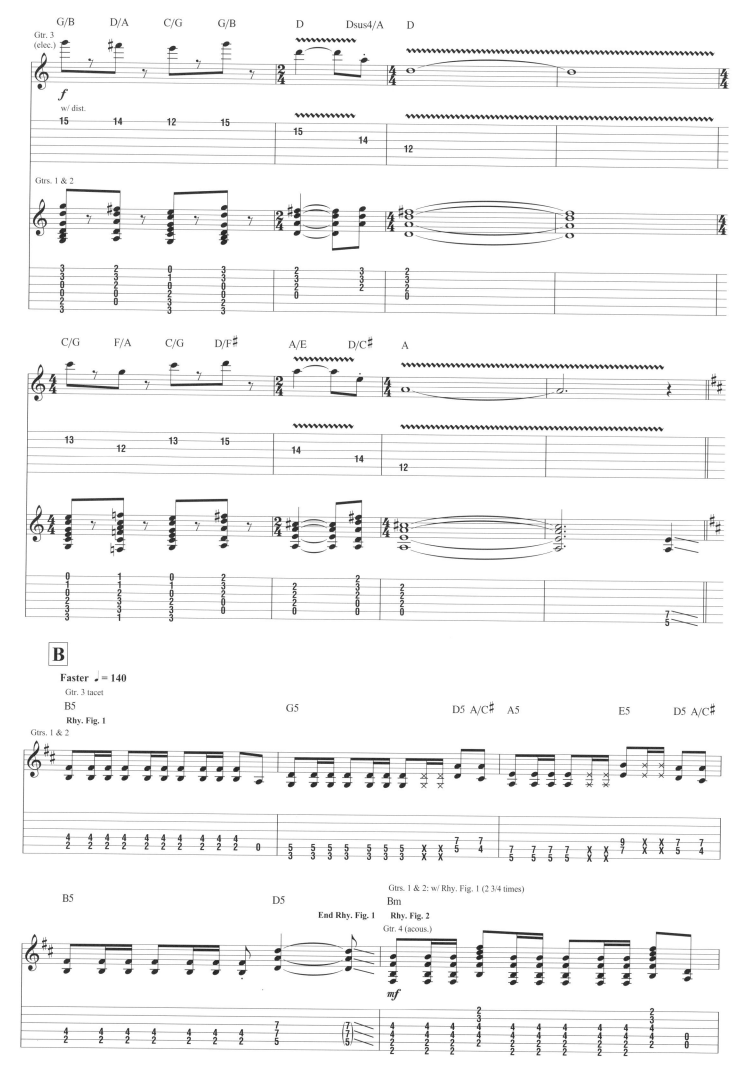

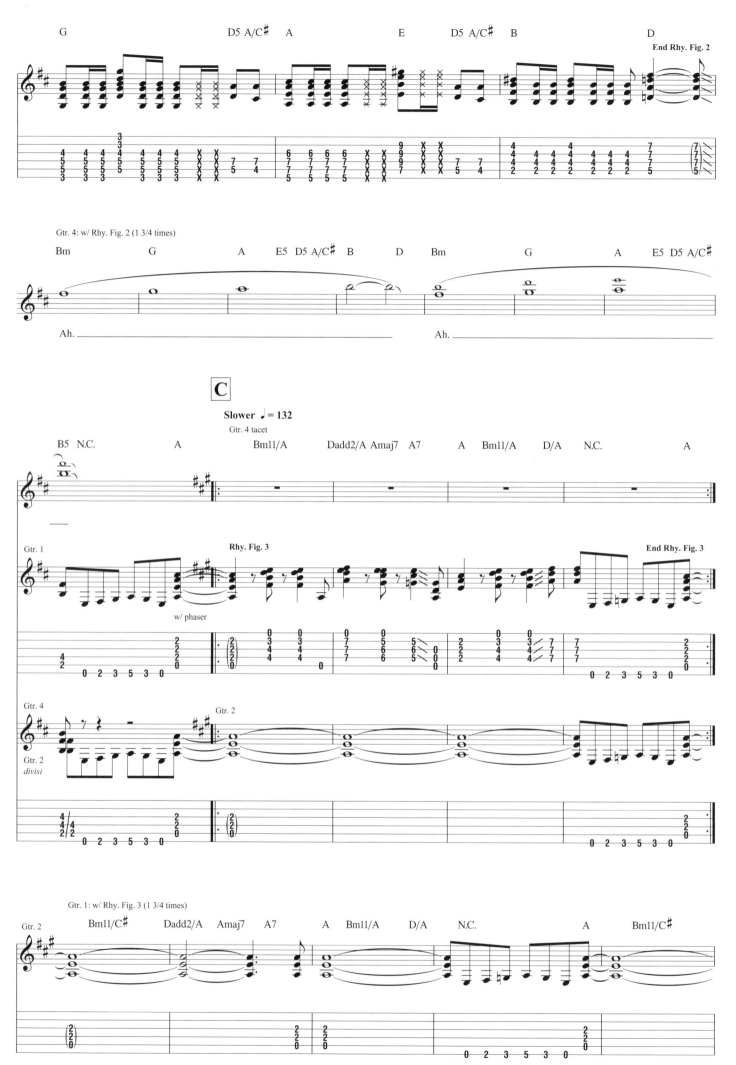

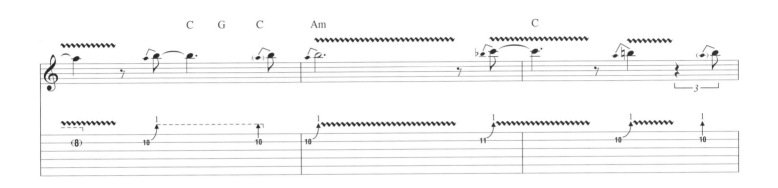

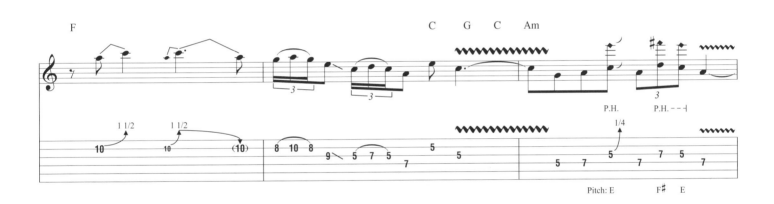

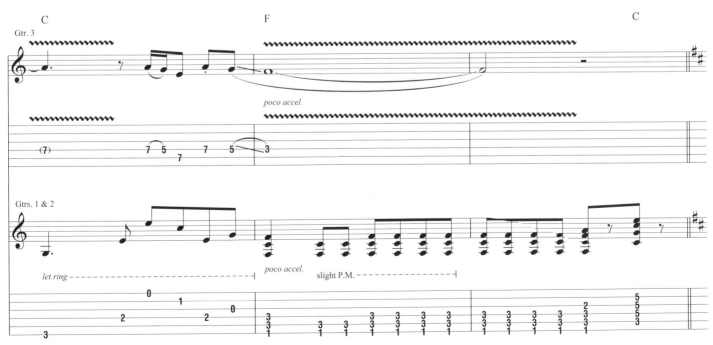

34

And the meek shall in-her-it the earth.

2112
II. Temples of Syrinx

Words and Music by Alex Lifeson, Geddy Lee and Neil Peart

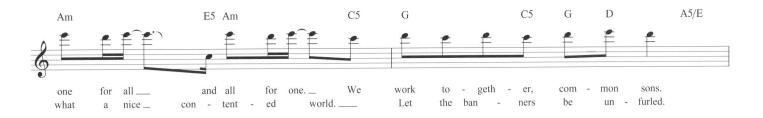

one for all ___ and all for one. We work to- geth - er, com - mon sons.
what a nice ___ con - tent - ed world. ___ Let the ban - ners be un - furled.

Nev - er need to won - der how or why.
Hold the Red Star proud - ly high in hand.

Gtr. 1

poco accel.

let ring – –

Chorus

♩ = 135

We ___ are ___ the Priests ___ of the Tem - ples of Syr - inx.

Rhy. Fig. 2

End Rhy. Fig. 2

let ring - - - - - -┤   *let ring - - - - - - - - - -┤*   *let ring - - - - - - - - - -┤*   *let ring –*

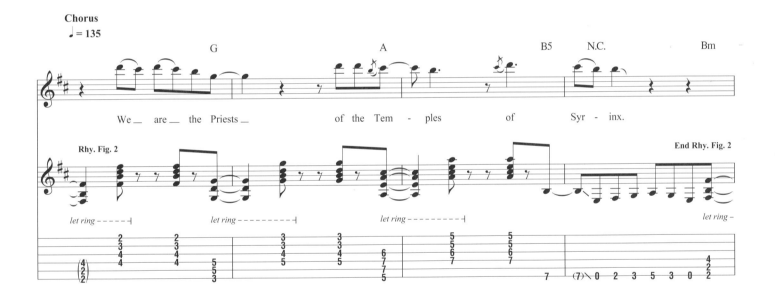

Gtr. 1: w/ Rhy. Fig. 2 (2 times)

{ Our great ___ }
{ Our ___ great } com - put - ers fill ___ the ___ hal - lowed ___ halls. _____

We ___ are ___ the Priests ___ of the Tem - ples of Syr - inx.

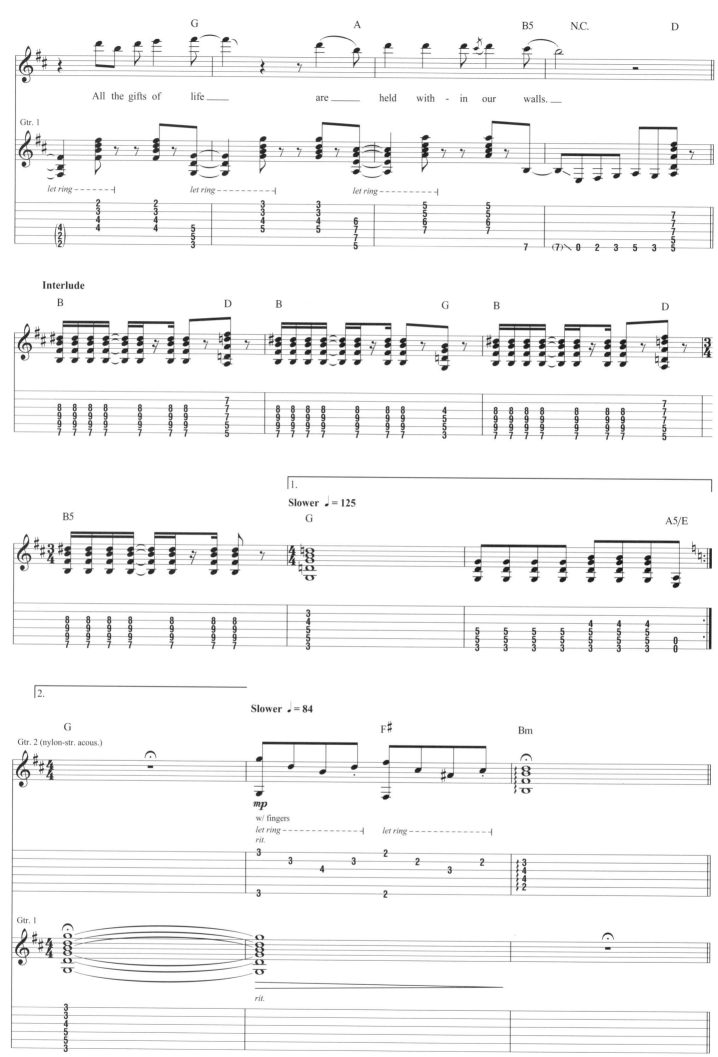

All the gifts of life ___ are ___ held with-in our walls. ___

Closer to the Heart

Words and Music by Alex Lifeson, Geddy Lee, Neil Peart and Peter Talbot

*Chord symbols reflect overall harmony.

**Composite arrangement

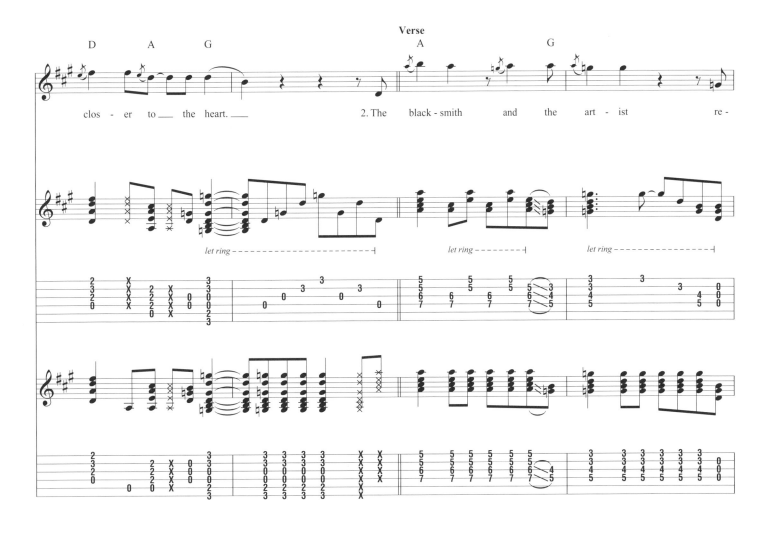

clos - er to __ the heart. __   2. The black - smith   and   the   art - ist   re -

flect it in __ their art. __   They forge their cre - a - tiv - i - ty

*Orchestral bells arr. for gtr.

**See top of first page of song for chord diagrams pertaining to rhythm slashes.

***Two gtrs. arr. for one.

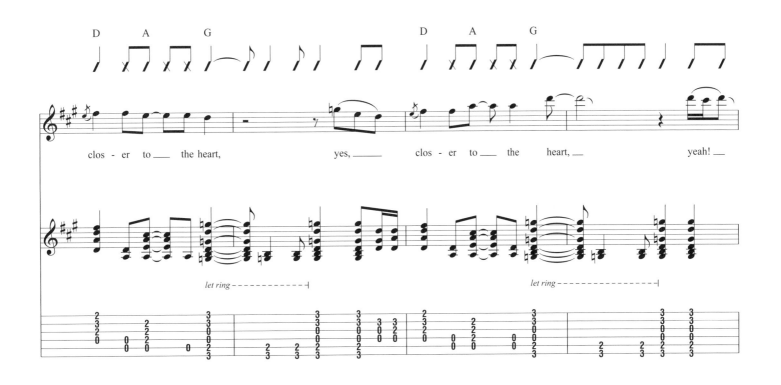

closer to ___ the heart,   yes, ___   clos - er to ___ the heart, ___   yeah! ___

let ring - - - - - - - - - - - ⌐   *let ring - - - - - - - - - - - - - - - ⌐*

Guitar Solo

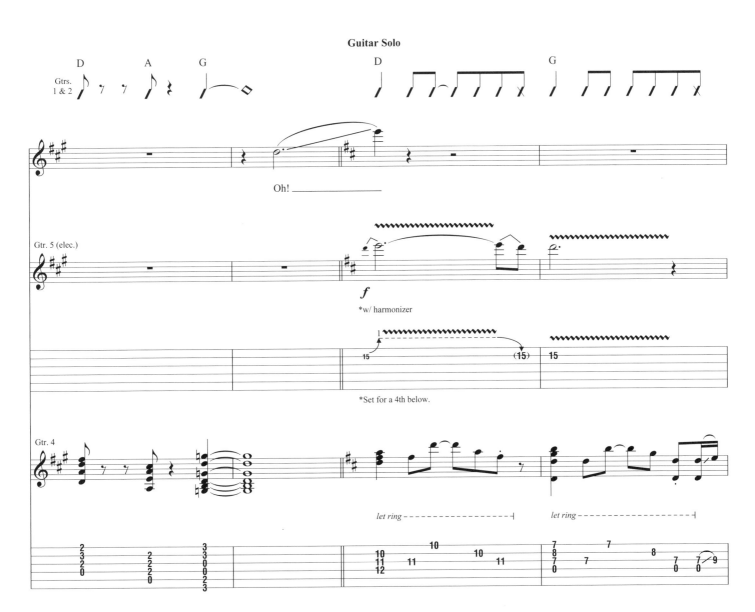

Oh! ___

*w/ harmonizer

*Set for a 4th below.

let ring - - - - - - - - - - ⌐   *let ring - - - - - - - - - - - ⌐*

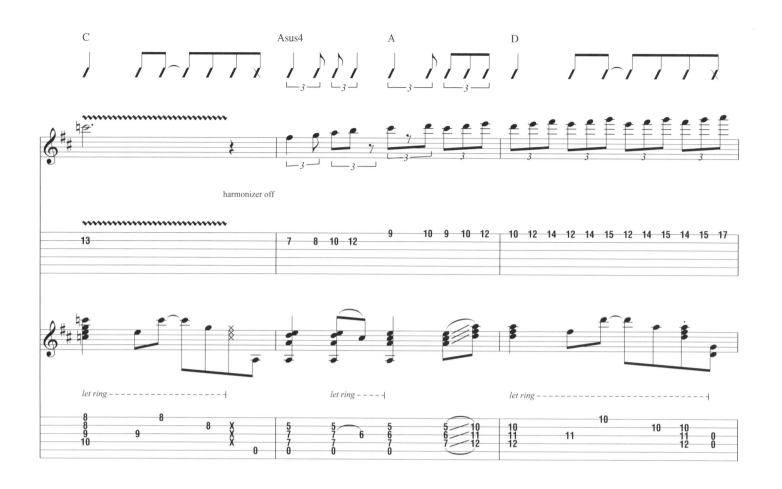

harmonizer off

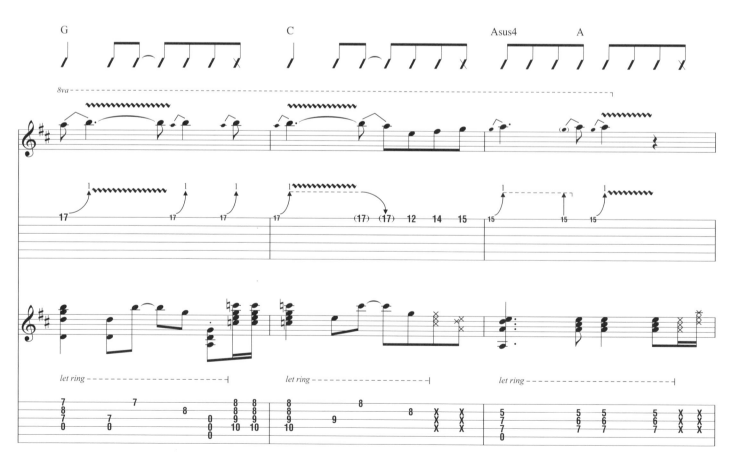

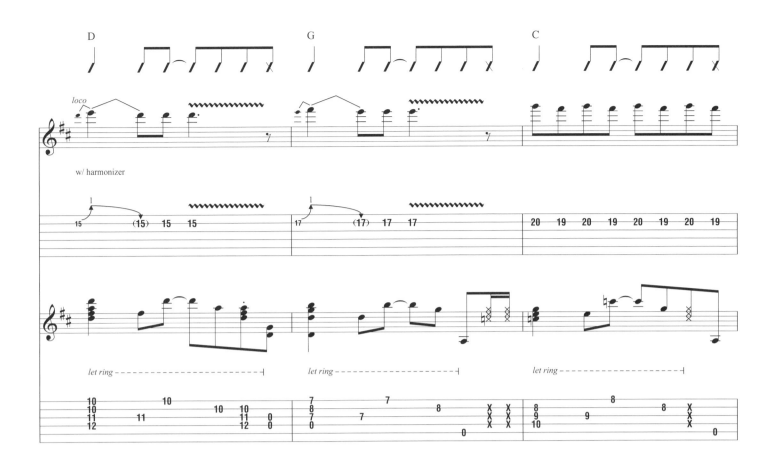

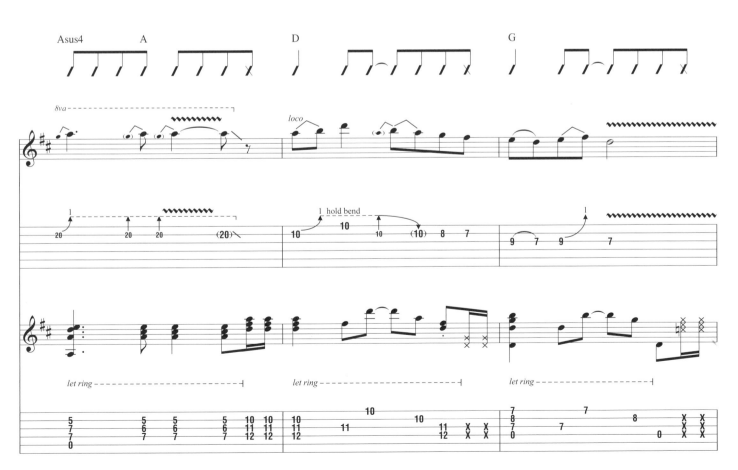

Interlude

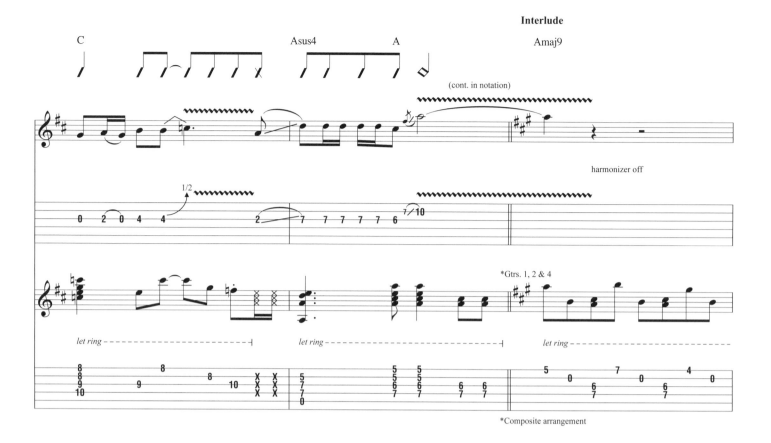

*Composite arrangement

I said, clos - er to ___ the heart. ___ Well, ___

Begin fade

clos - er to ___ the heart, ___ yeah! Clos - er ___ to your ___

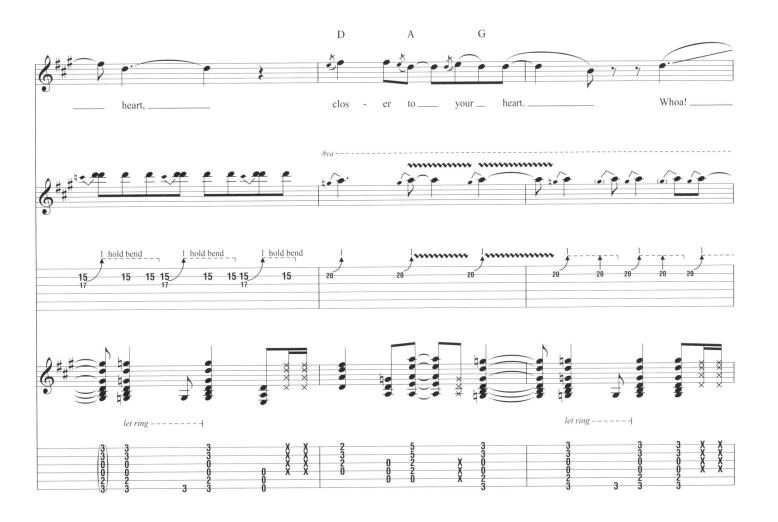

heart,   clos - er to   your   heart.   Whoa!

Fade out

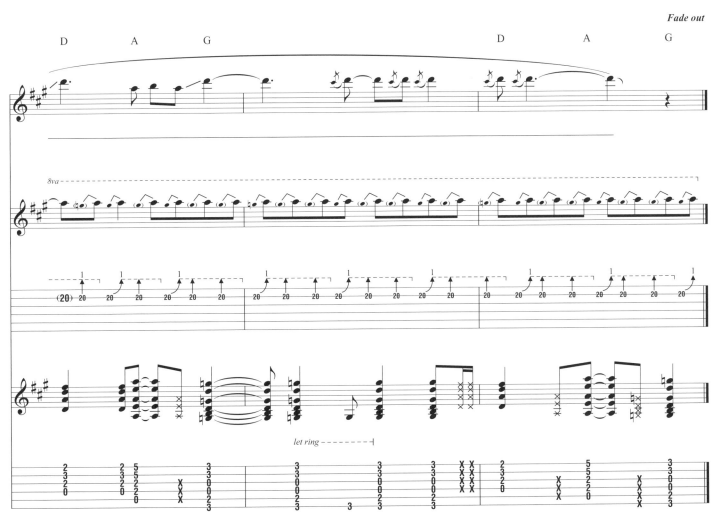

The Trees

Words and Music by Alex Lifeson, Geddy Lee and Neil Peart

*Chord symbols reflect overall harmony.

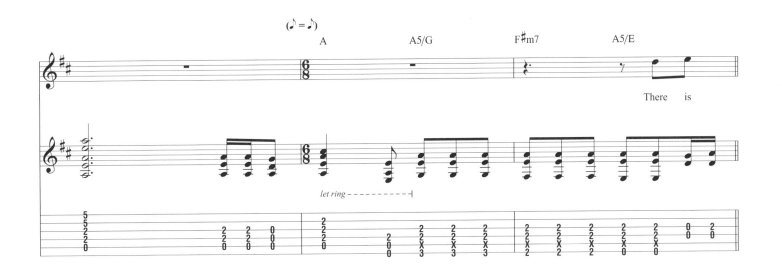

Chorus

trou - ble in the for - est, and the crea - tures all have fled as the

ma - ples scream, "Op - pres - sion!" and the oaks just __ shake their __ heads.

Interlude

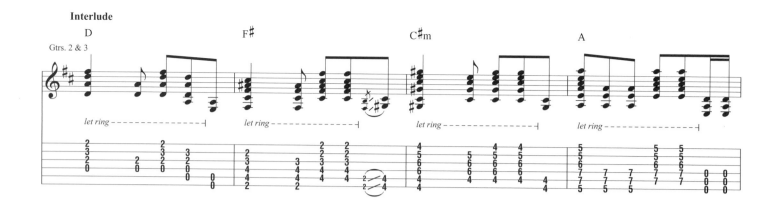

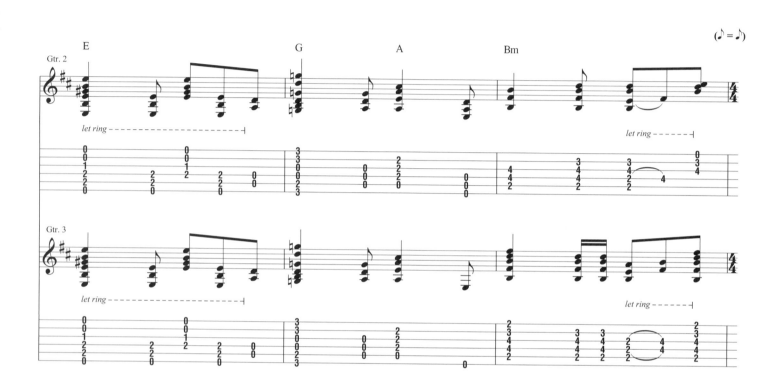

Interlude

Gtrs. 2 & 3 tacet

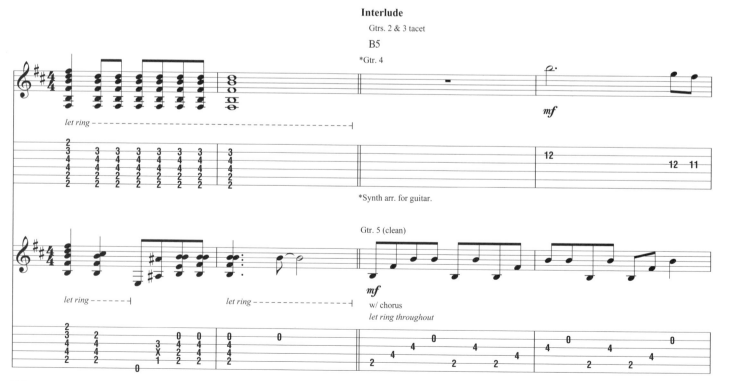

*Synth arr. for guitar.

54

*Gtr. 6 (clean), w/ chorus; fade in to *mf* next 4 meas.

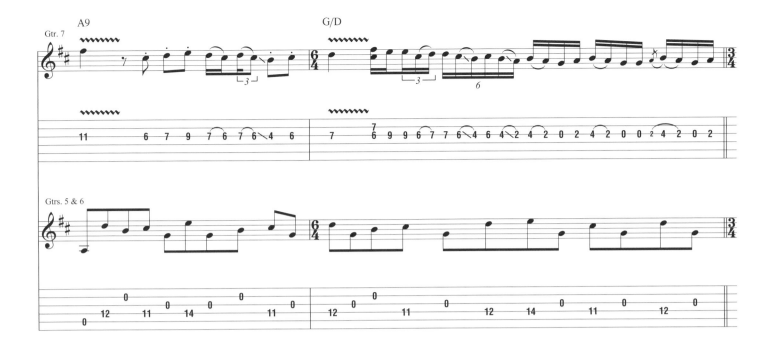

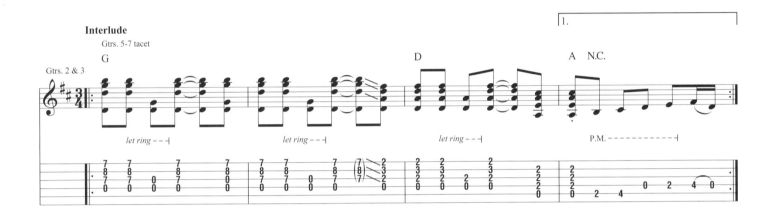

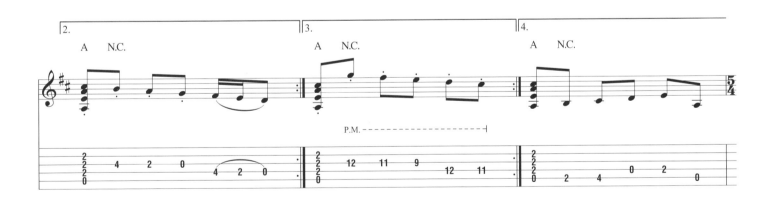

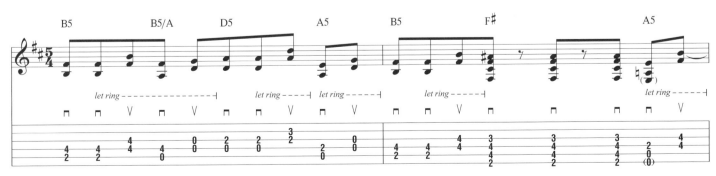

*Gtrs. 5 & 6 to left of slash in tab.

Spirit of Radio

Words and Music by Alex Lifeson, Geddy Lee and Neil Peart

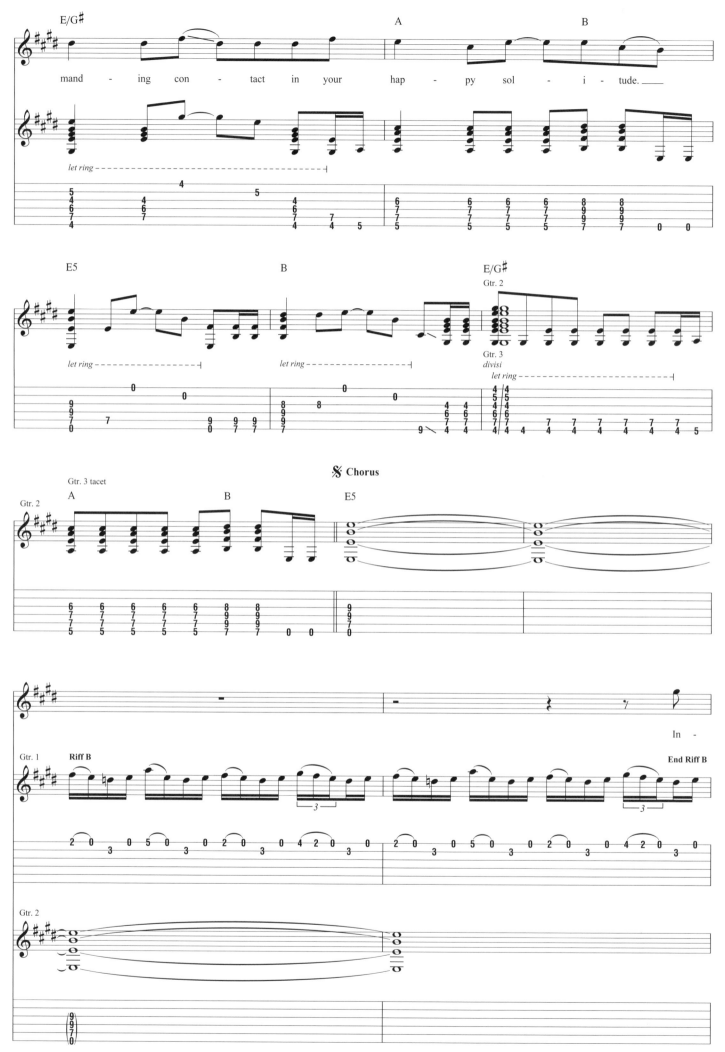

1st time, Gtr. 1: w/ Riff B (6 times)
2nd time, Gtr. 1: w/ Riff B (5 times)
Gtr. 2 tacet

vis - i - ble air - waves crack - le with life, ___ bright an - ten - nae bris -

- tle with the en - er - gy. E -

mo - tion - al feed - back on a time - less wave - length bear - ing a gift ___ be - yond ___

To Coda ⊕

price, al - most ___ free.

Verse

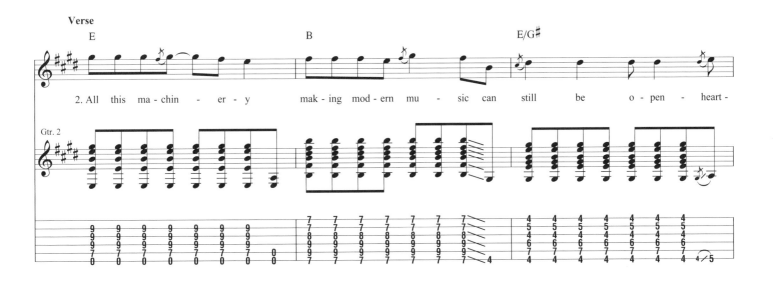

2. All this ma - chin - er - y mak - ing mod - ern mu - sic can still be o - pen - heart -

Gtr. 2

ed. Not so cold - ly chart - ed, it's real - ly just a ques - tion of your

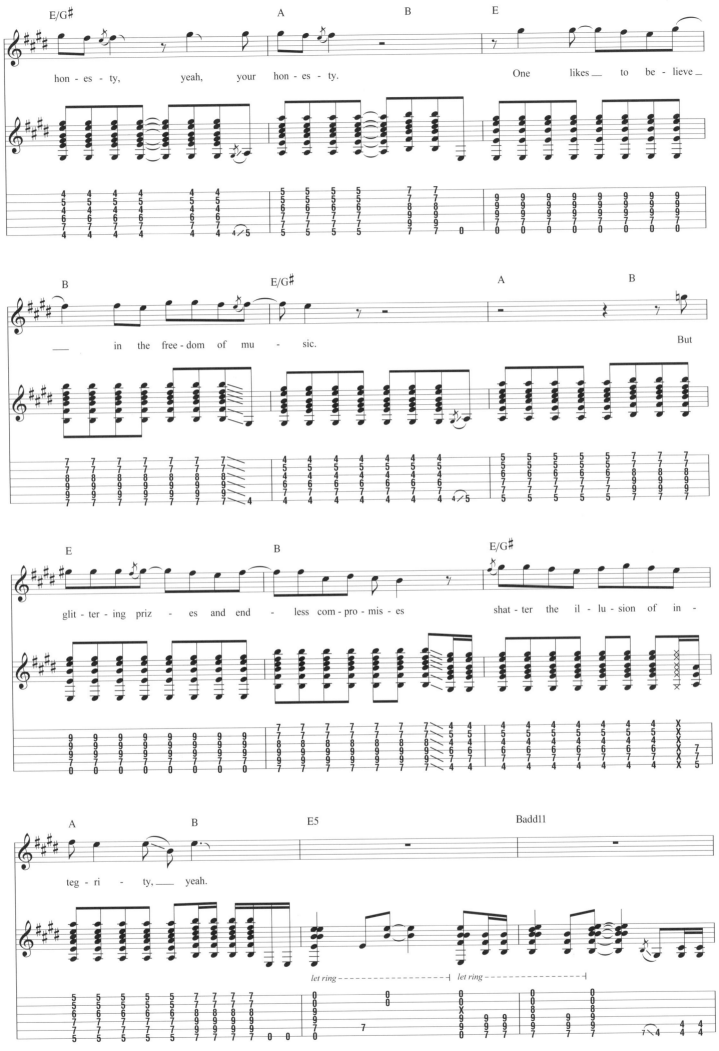

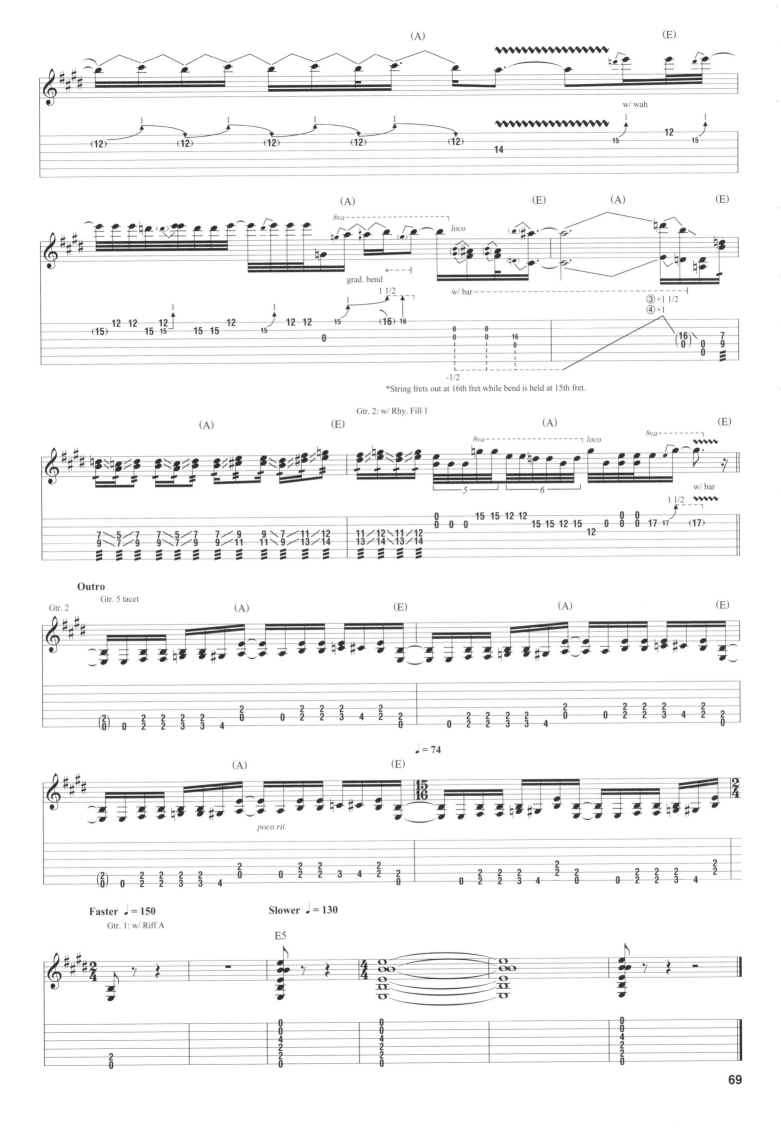

*String frets out at 16th fret while bend is held at 15th fret.

Freewill

Words and Music by Alex Lifeson, Geddy Lee and Neil Peart

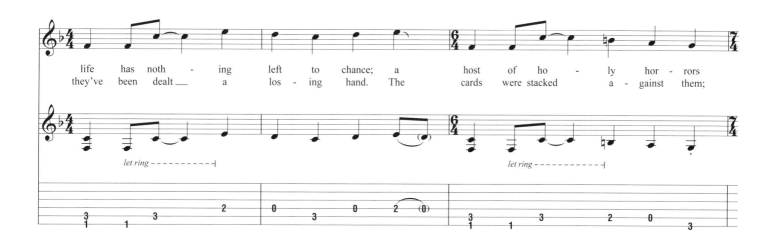

life has noth - ing left to chance; a host of ho - ly hor - rors
they've been dealt ___ a los - ing hand. The cards were stacked a - gainst them;

let ring

to di - rect our aim - less dance. _____
they weren't born ___ in ___ Lo - tus - Land.

let ring

let ring

Pre-Chorus
Half-time feel

Bm11   B♭maj7♯11

A plan - et of _____ play - things, __ we
All pre - or - dained, __ a

Rhy. Fig. 1

let ring

§ § **Chorus**

End half-time feel

Guitar Solo

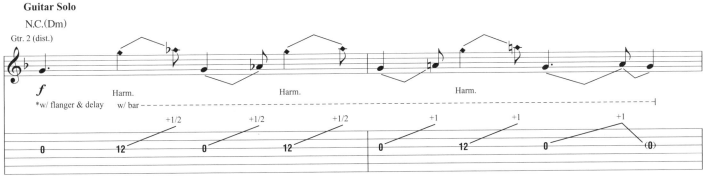

*Delay set for quarter-note regeneration.

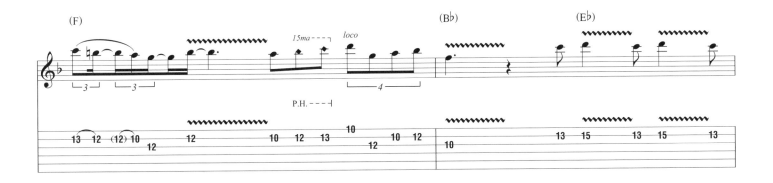

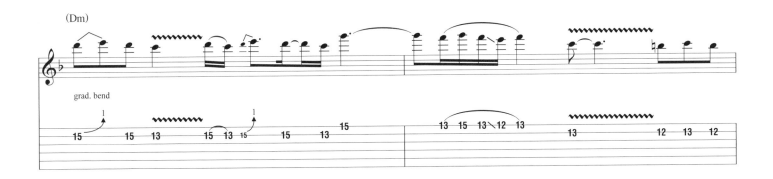

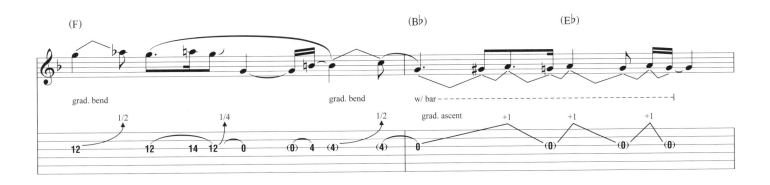

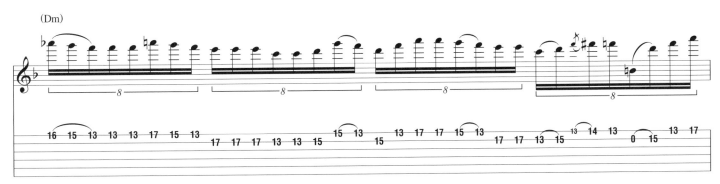

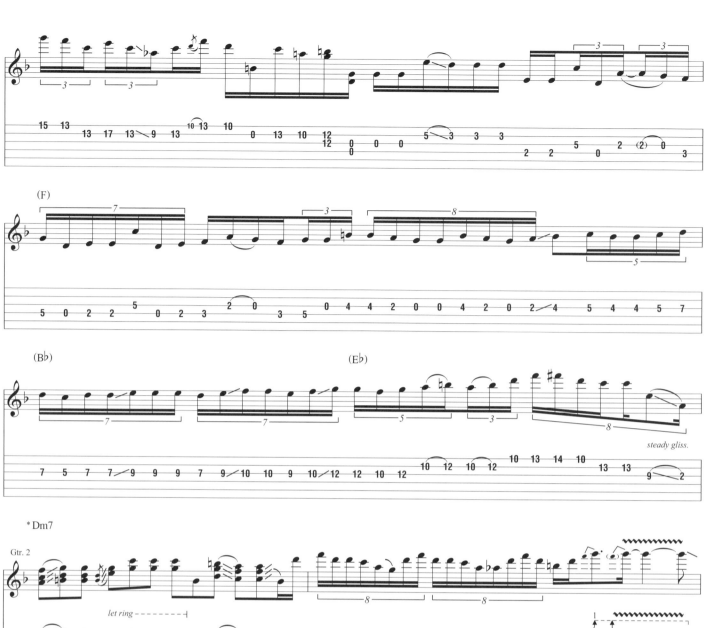

*Chord symbols reflect overall harmony, next 8 meas.

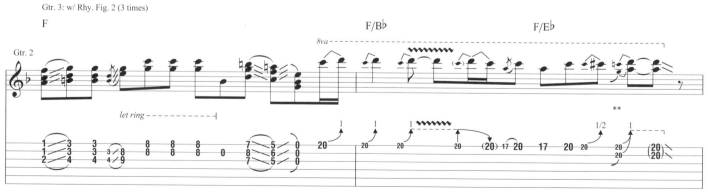

**Catch 2nd string with bending finger.

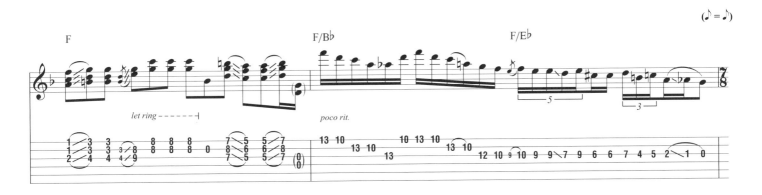

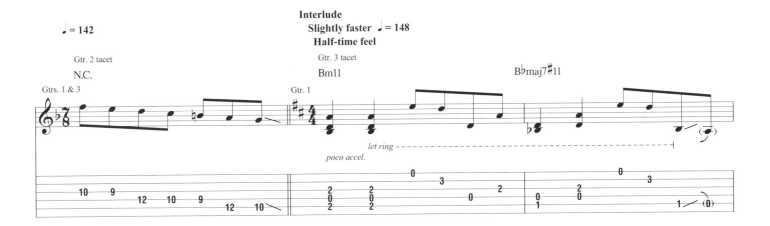

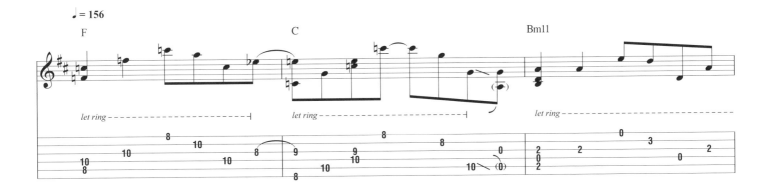

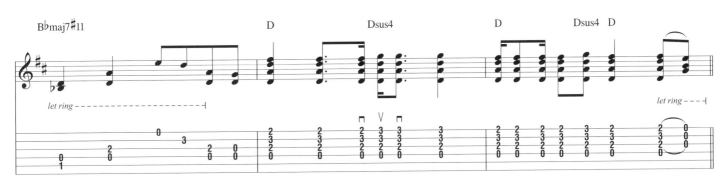

Gtr. 1: w/ Rhy. Fig. 1

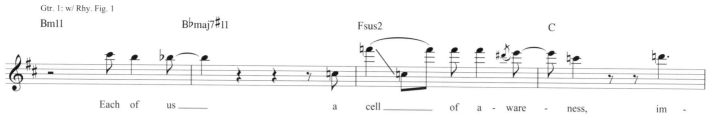

Each of us _____ a cell _____ of a - ware - ness, im -

per - fect and _____ in - com - plete. _____

Ge - net - ic blends _____ with un - cer - tain ends _____ on a

D.S.S. al Coda 2
End half-time feel

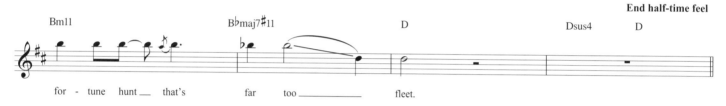

for - tune hunt _____ that's far too _____ fleet.

Coda 2

Outro

will.

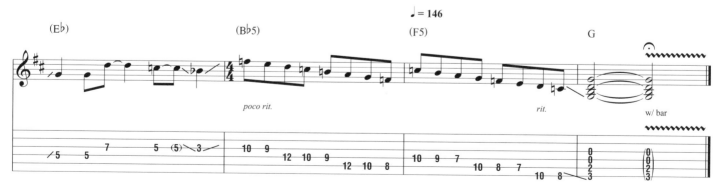

Limelight

Words and Music by Alex Lifeson, Geddy Lee and Neil Peart

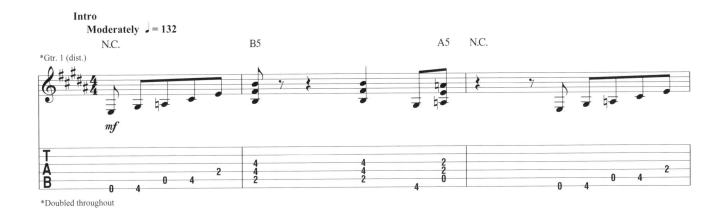

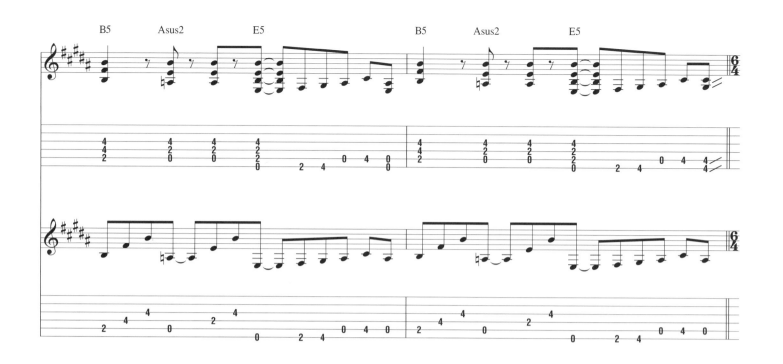

Verse

1. Liv - ing on __ a light - ed __ stage ap - proach - es the un - real, for

those who think and feel, in touch with some re-al-i-ty be-yond the gild-ed cage.

Cast in this un-like-ly role, ill e-quipped to act, with

in-suf-fi-cient tact. One must put up bar-ri-ers to

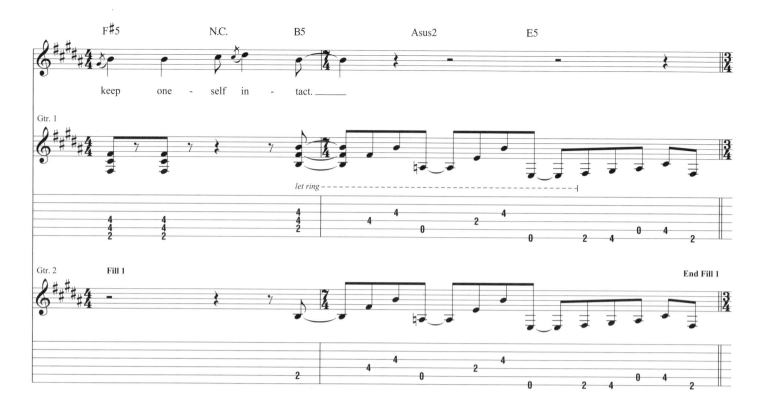

keep one - self in - tact. _____

%% Chorus

Liv - ing in ___ the lime - light, the u - ni - ver - sal dream, ___ for ___

*Gtr. 3 (slight dist.): w/ chorus, played *mf*,
Composite arrangement

**Bass plays E.

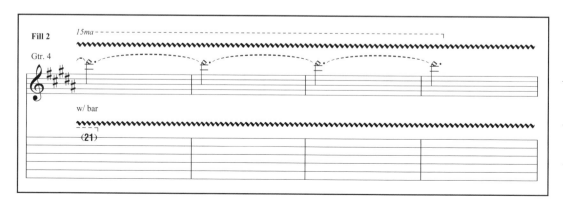

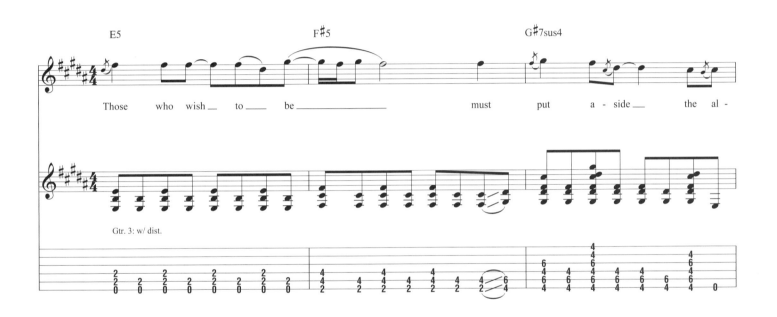

To Coda 1
To Coda 2

real re - al - tion, the un - der - ly - ing theme.

Gtr. 3: w/ slight dist.

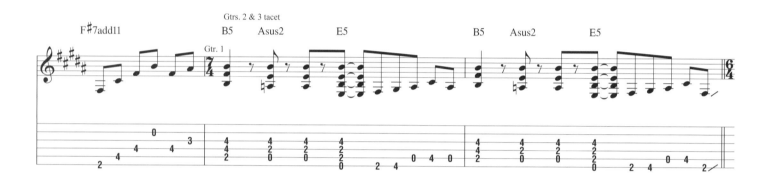

Gtrs. 2 & 3 tacet

Gtr. 1

Verse

Gtr. 1: w/ Rhy. Fig. 1
Gtr. 2: w/ Rhy. Fig. 1A (1 4/7 times)

2. Liv - ing in __ a fish - eye __ lens, caught in the cam - 'ra __ eye, __ I

have no heart to __ lie. __ I can't pre - tend __ a stran - ger is a

long a - wait - ed friend. _____

All the world's in - deed a stage, we are mere - ly play - ers, per -

form - ers and por - tray - ers. Each an - oth - er's au - di - ence out -

D.S. al Coda 1

side the gild - ed cage.

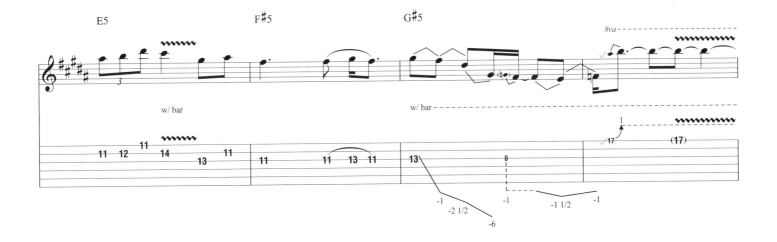

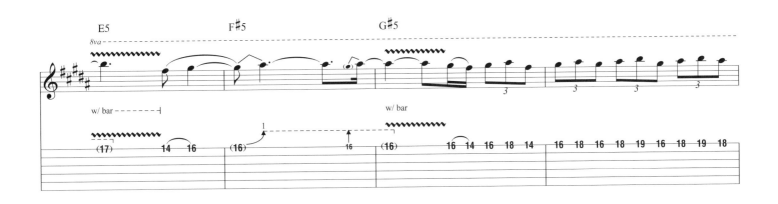

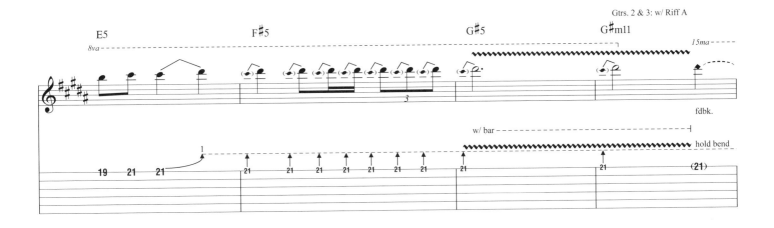

D.S. al Coda 2

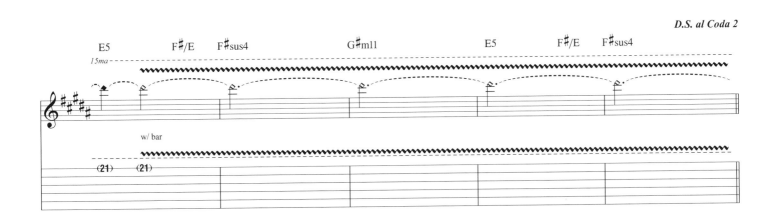

The real re-la-tion, the un-der-ly-ing theme.

Tom Sawyer

Words and Music by Alex Lifeson, Geddy Lee, Neil Peart and Pye Dubois

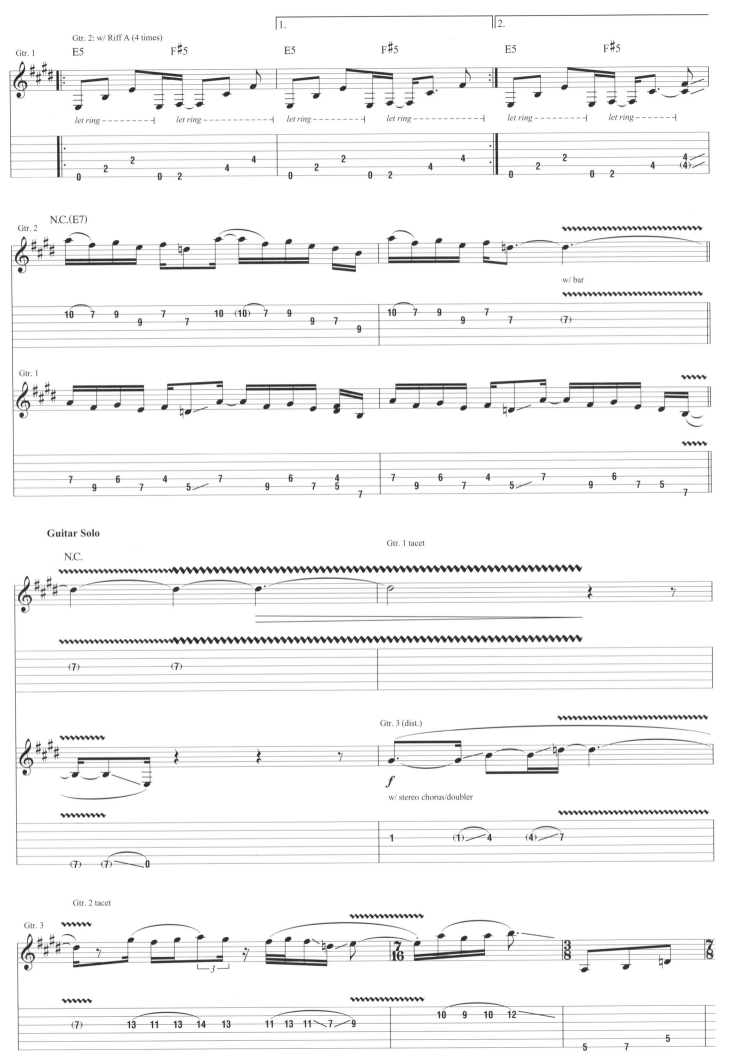

Red Barchetta

Words and Music by Alex Lifeson, Geddy Lee and Neil Peart

1. My

Verse

Gtrs. 2 & 3: w/ Riff A (1 1/2 times)

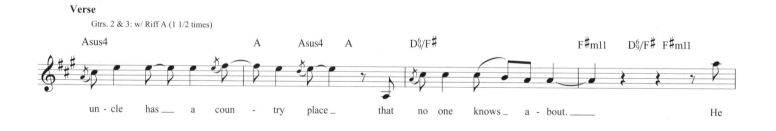

un - cle has ___ a coun - try place ___ that no one knows ___ a - bout. ____ He

says it used ___ to be _____ a farm, ___ be - fore the Mo - tor Law. ____ And on

Sun - days, I e - lude ____ the "Eyes," ___ and hop the Tur - bine Freight ___ to

far out - side the Wi - re where my ____ white-haired un - cle waits. ___

Interlude

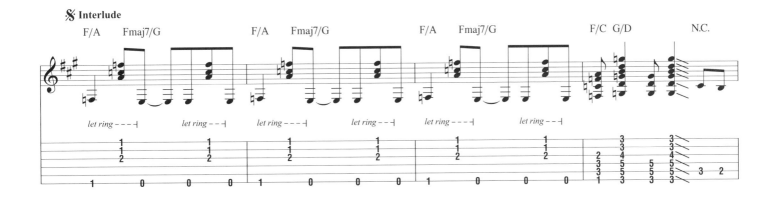

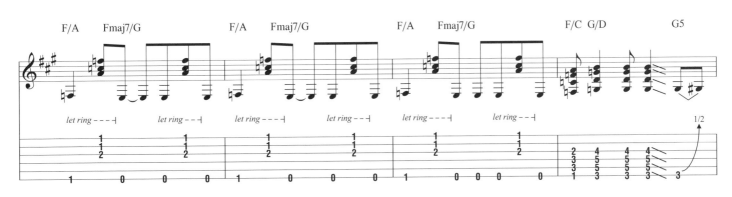

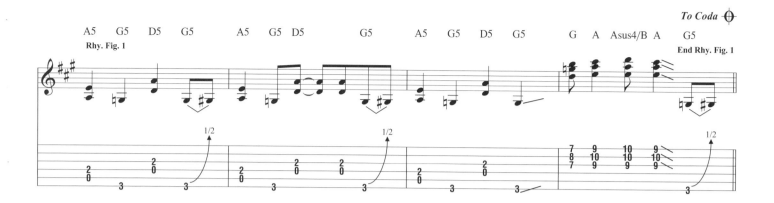

Chorus

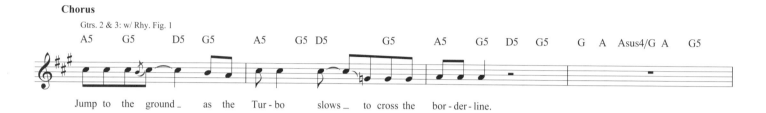

Jump to the ground _ as the Tur - bo slows _ to cross the bor - der - line.

Run like the wind _ as ex - cite - ment shiv - ers up and down my spine. But

Bridge

down in his barn, _ my un - cle pre - served _ for me an old ma - chine _ for fif - ty - odd years. To

fi - re up ___ the will - ing en - gine, re - spond - ing with a roar!

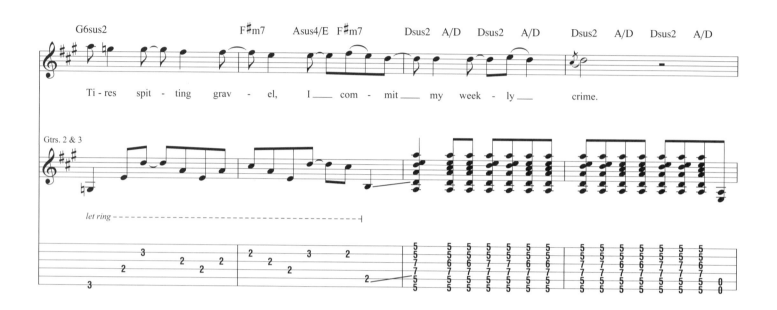

Ti - res spit - ting grav - el, I ___ com - mit ___ my week - ly ___ crime.

Interlude

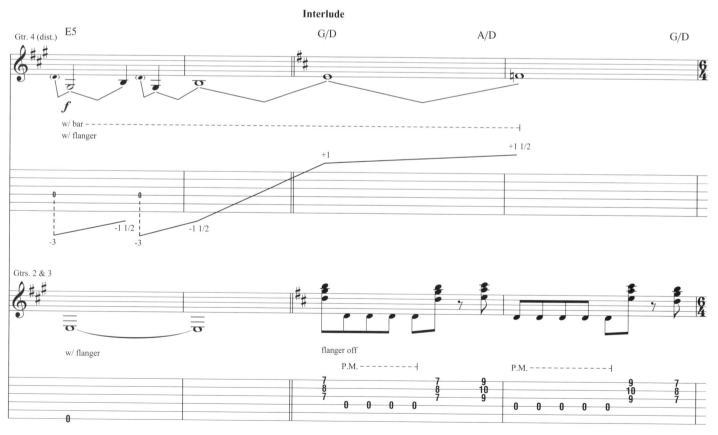

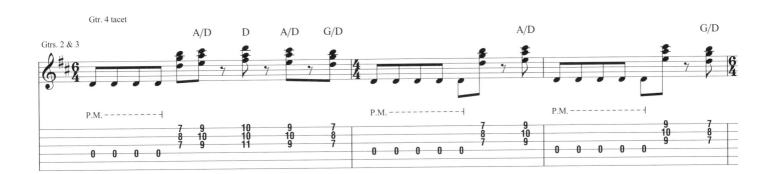

Bridge

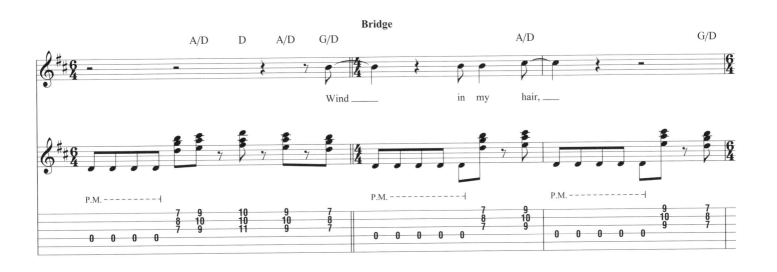

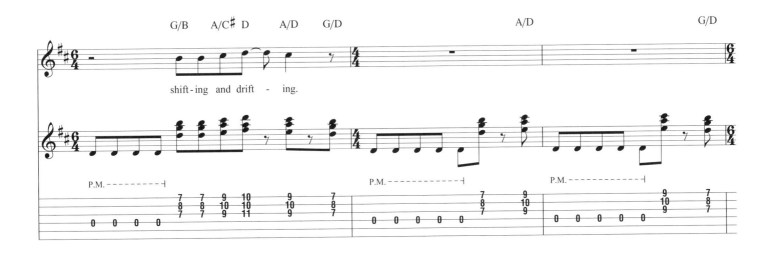

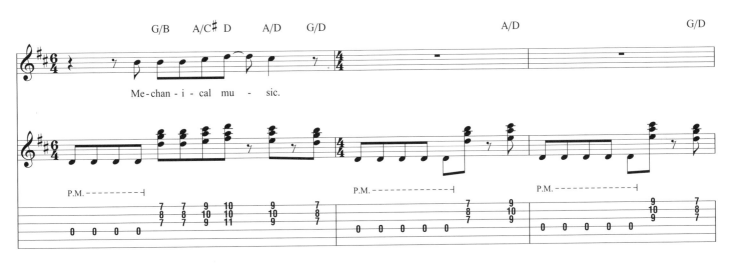

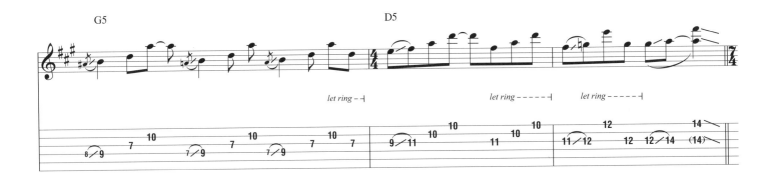

Interlude

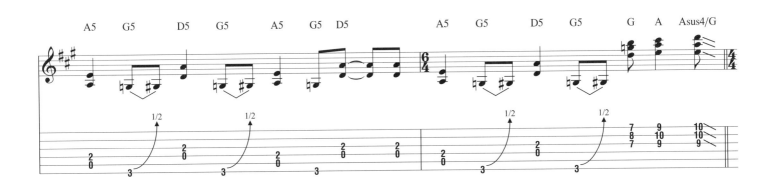

Verse

3. Sud-den-ly __ a-head __ of me, __ a-cross the moun-tain - side, __ a

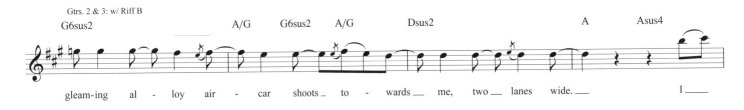

gleam-ing al - loy air - car shoots to - wards __ me, two __ lanes wide. __ I __

spin a - round __ with shriek-ing tires __ to run the dead-ly race, go __

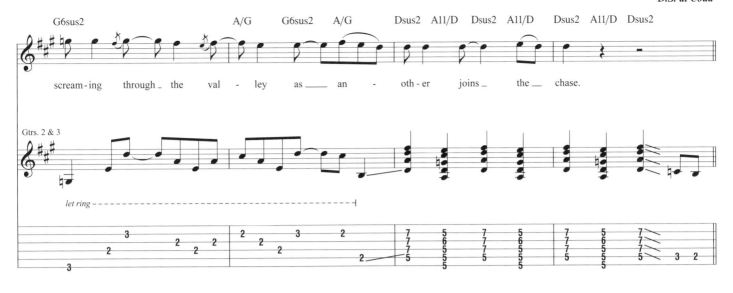

G6sus2 — A/G — G6sus2 — A/G — Dsus2 — A11/D — Dsus2 — A11/D — Dsus2 — A11/D — Dsus2

scream-ing through the val-ley as ___ an - oth-er joins ___ the ___ chase.

Gtrs. 2 & 3

let ring

Coda

Chorus

Gtrs. 2 & 3: w/ Rhy. Fig. 1 (1 3/4 times)

A5 — G5 — D5 — G5 — A5 — G5 — D5 — G5 — A5 — G5 — D5 — G5 — G — A — Asus4/G — A — G5

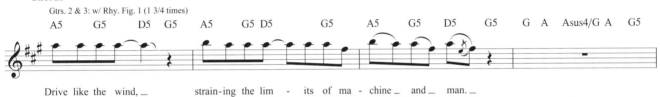

Drive like the wind, ___ strain-ing the lim - its of ma-chine ___ and ___ man. ___

A5 — G5 — D5 — G5 — A5 — G5 — D5 — G5 — A5 — G5 — D5 — G5 — G — A — Asus4/G — A

Gtrs. 2 & 3: w/ Rhy. Fill 1

Laugh-ing out loud with fear and hope, ___ I've got a des-per-ate ___ plan. At the

Bridge

Gtrs. 2 & 3: w/ Rhy. Fig. 2

F/A — Fsus2/G — C — F/A — Fsus2/G — C — F/A — Fsus2/G — C/G — F/C G/D

one-lane ___ bridge, ___ I leave the gi-ants strand - ed at the riv-er-side, ___ race ___

F/A — Fsus2/G — C — F/A — Fsus2/G — C — F/A — Fsus2/G — C

back to the farm ___ to dream with my un - cle at the fi - re - side.

Gtrs. 2 & 3

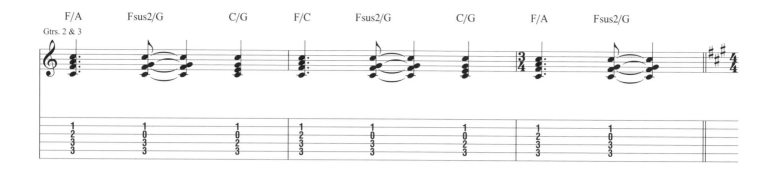

Interlude

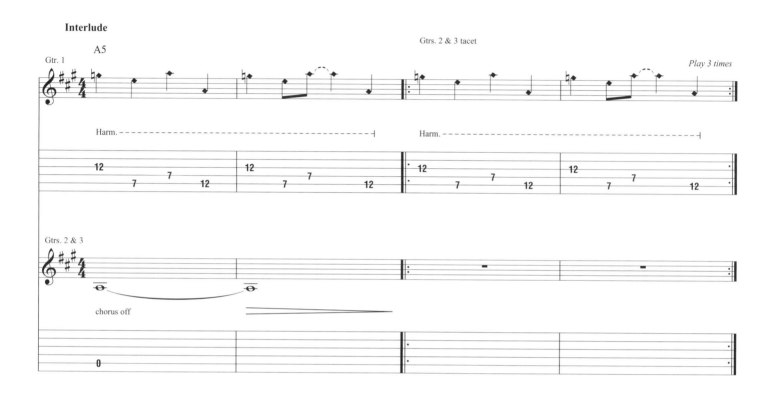

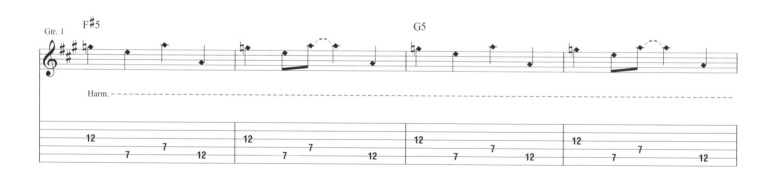

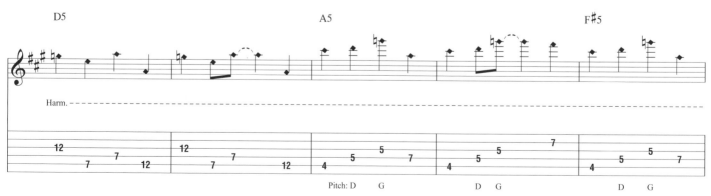

Pitch: D   G   D   G   D   G

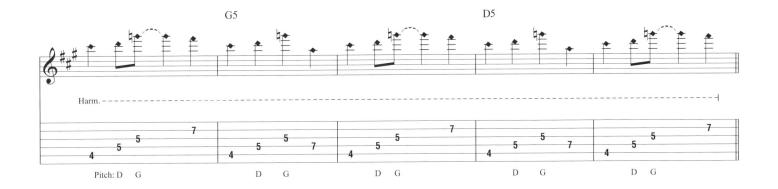

Outro
Half-time feel

Begin fade

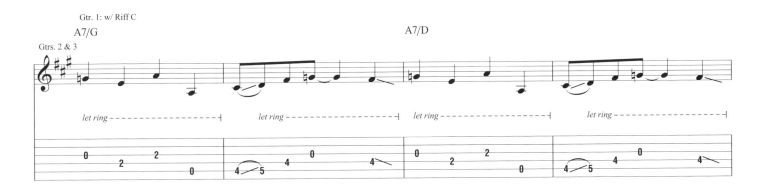

Fade out

New World Man

Words and Music by Alex Lifeson, Geddy Lee and Neil Peart

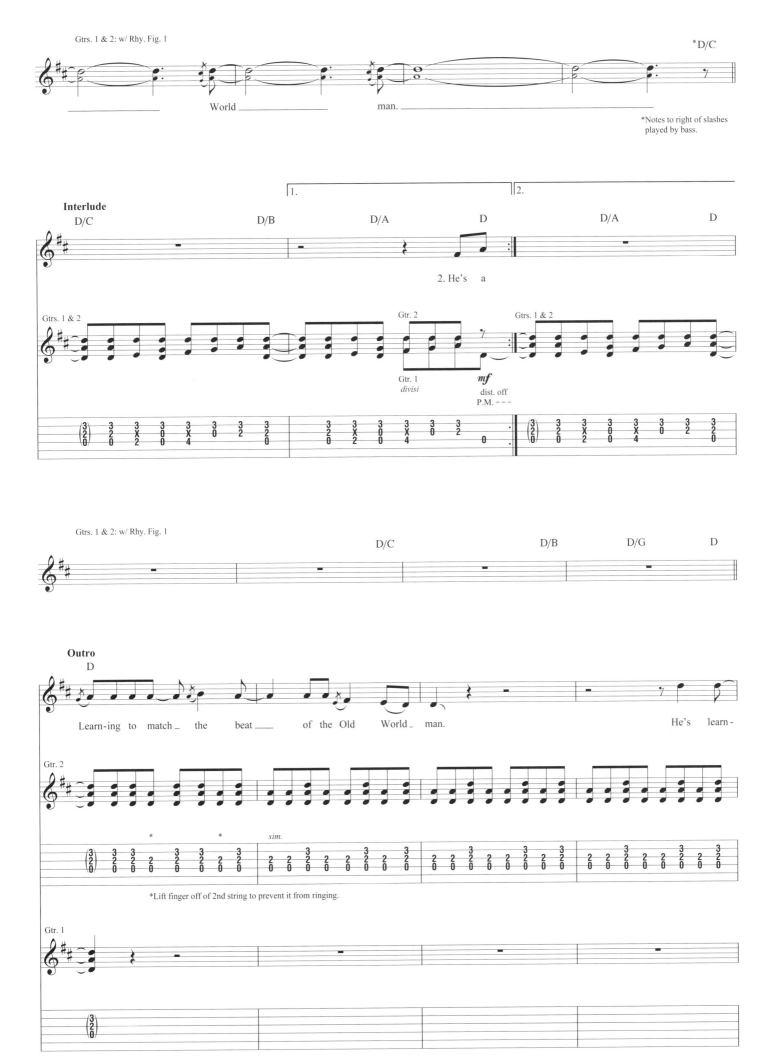

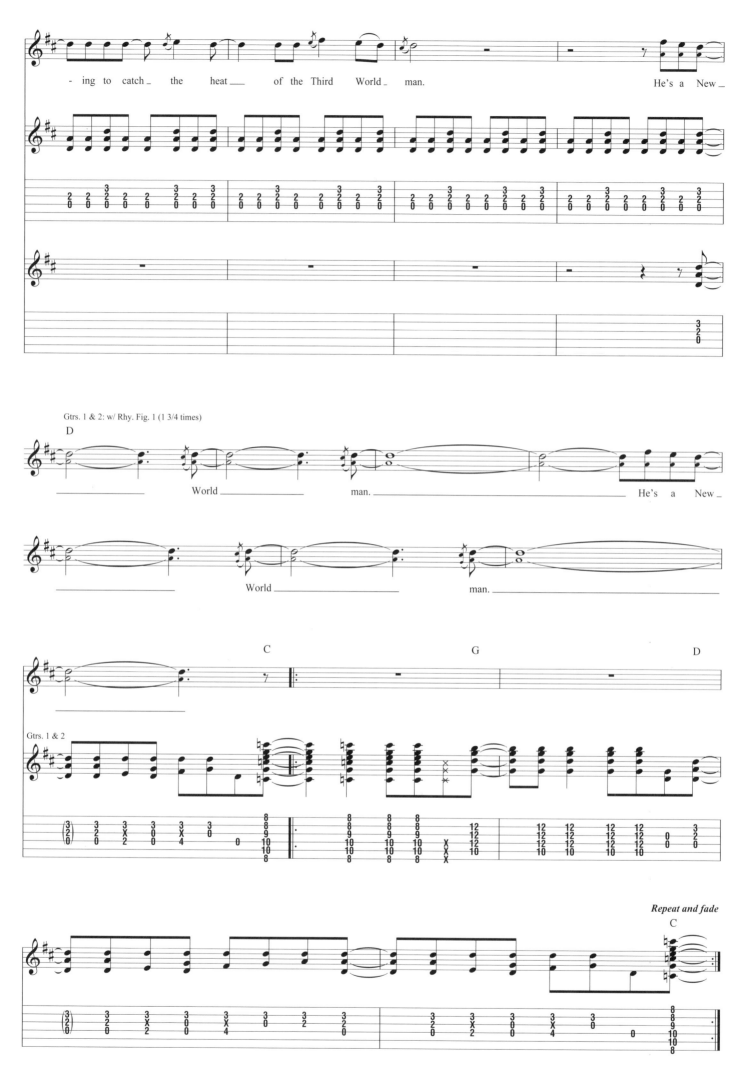

Subdivisions

Words and Music by Alex Lifeson, Geddy Lee and Neil Peart

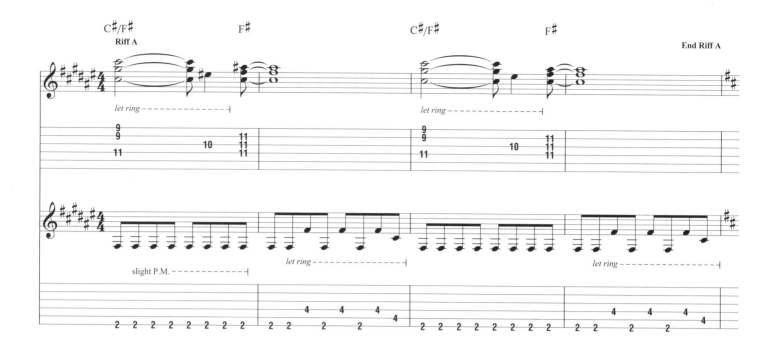

117

in be - tween the bright lights and the far un - lit un - known.
tached and sub - di - vid - ed in the mass pro - duc - tion zone.
lit up like a fi - re - fly, just to feel the liv - ing night.

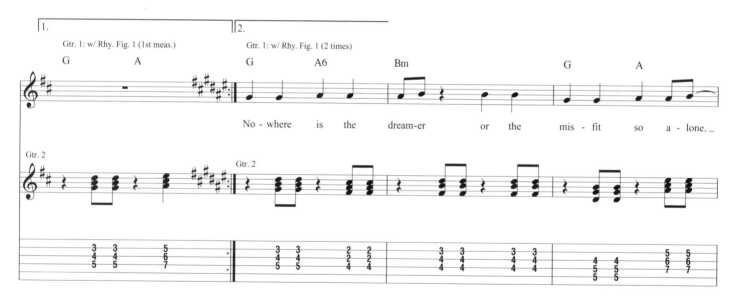

No - where is the dream - er or the mis - fit so a - lone.

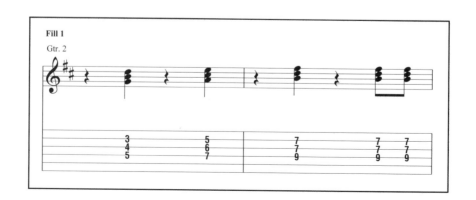

Fill 1
Gtr. 2

118

sub - urbs   have __   no   charms   to   soothe __   the   rest - less   dreams __   of   youth. _____

Synth Solo

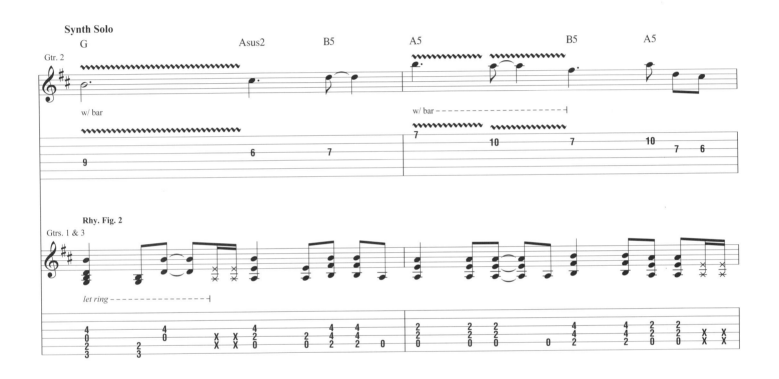

Rhy. Fig. 2

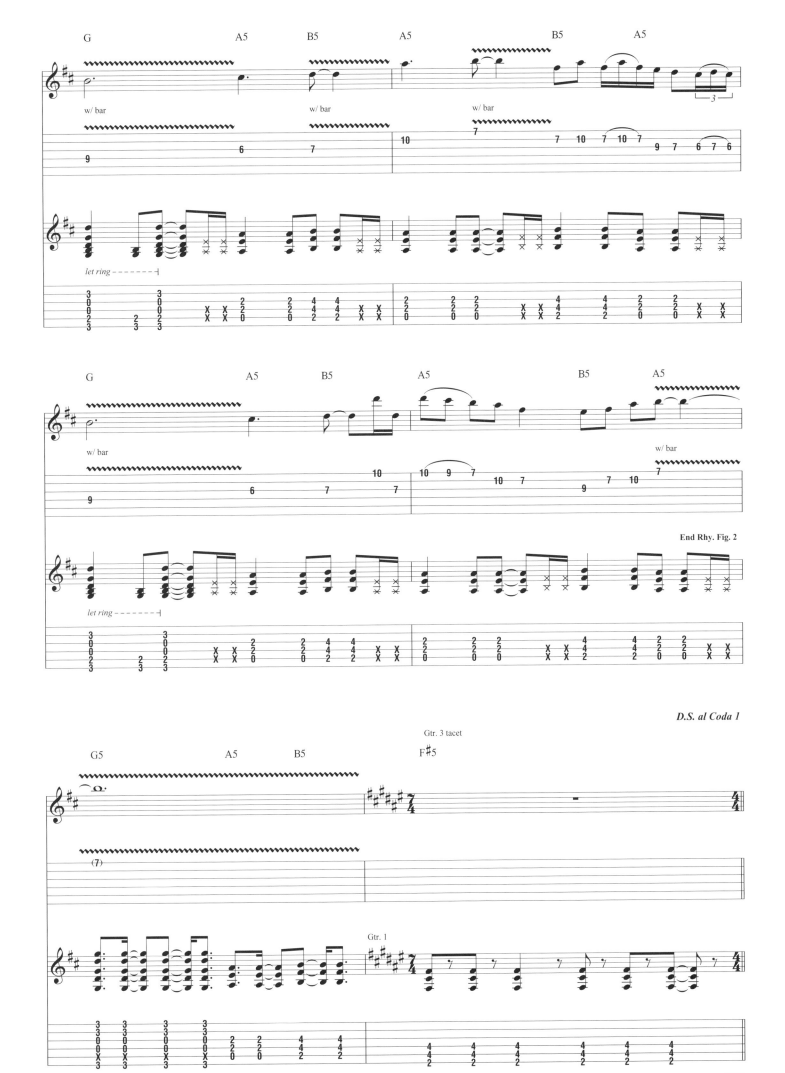

Lyrics: Some - where out of a mem-o - ry ___ of light-ed streets ___ on qui - et nights... ___

Coda 2

Synth Solo

Gtrs. 1 & 3: w/ Rhy. Fig. 2

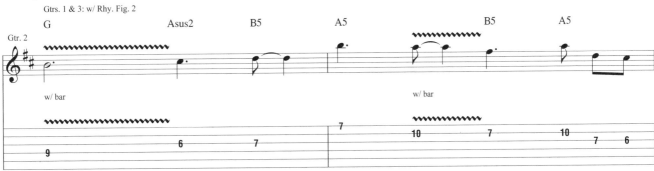

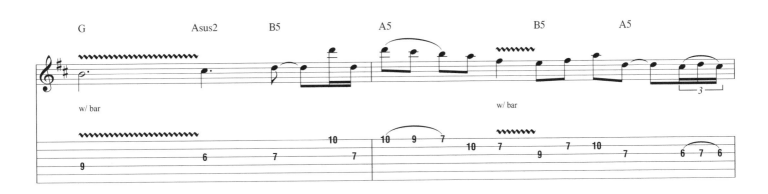

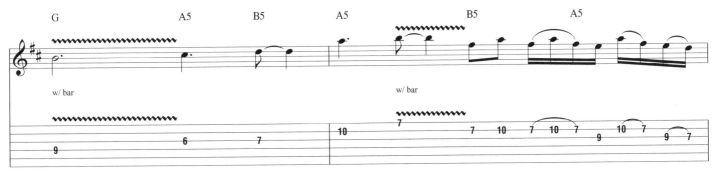

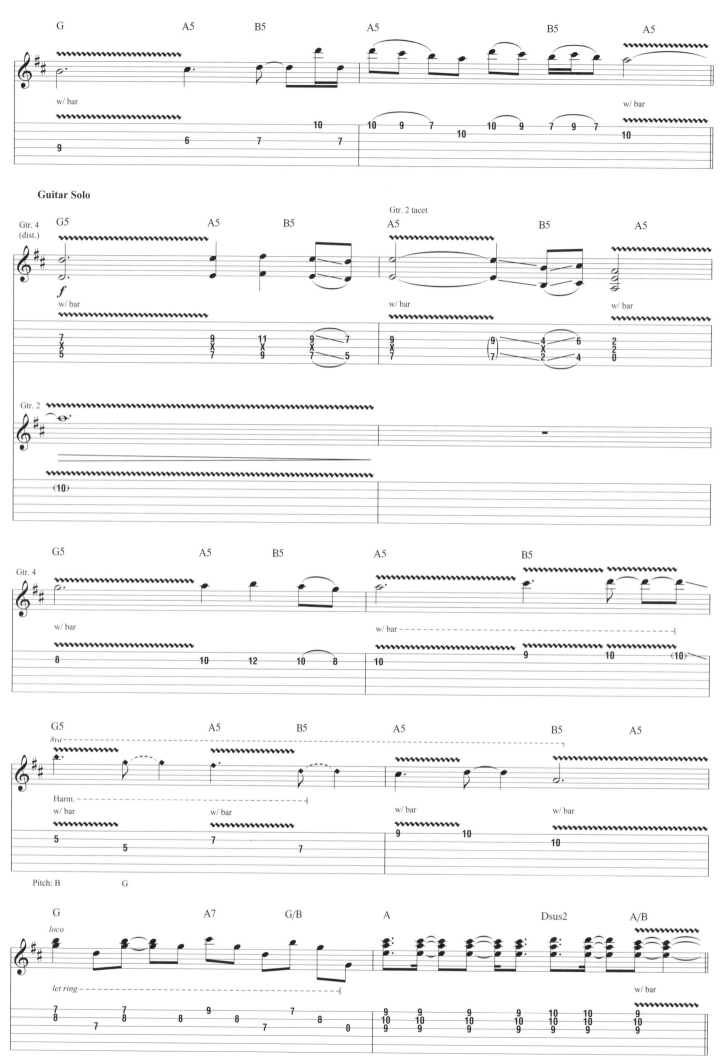

Guitar Solo

Distant Early Warning

Words and Music by Alex Lifeson, Geddy Lee and Neil Peart

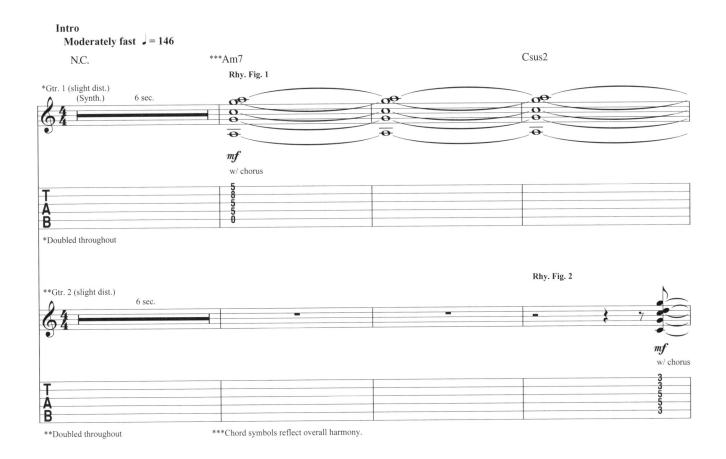

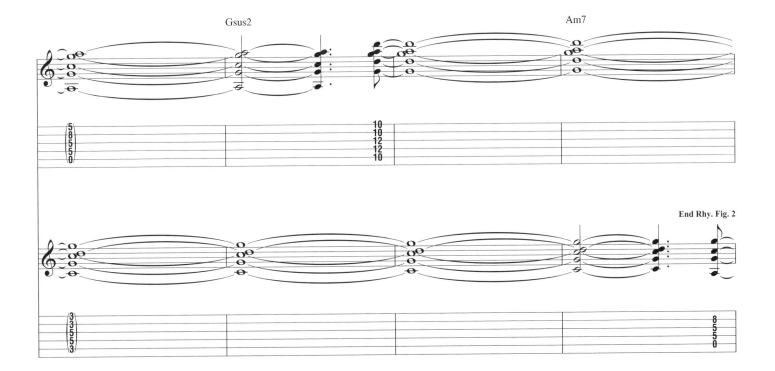

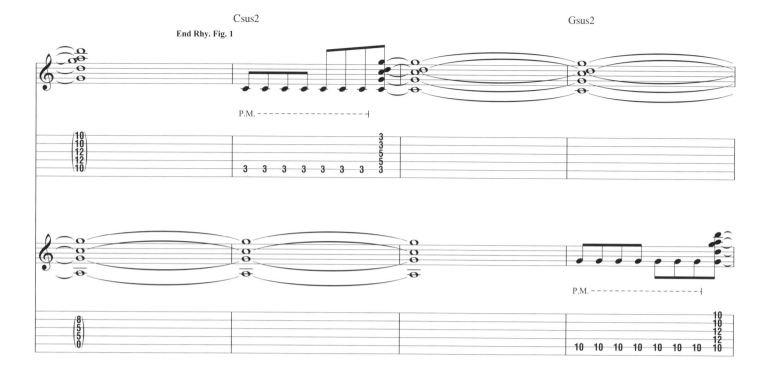

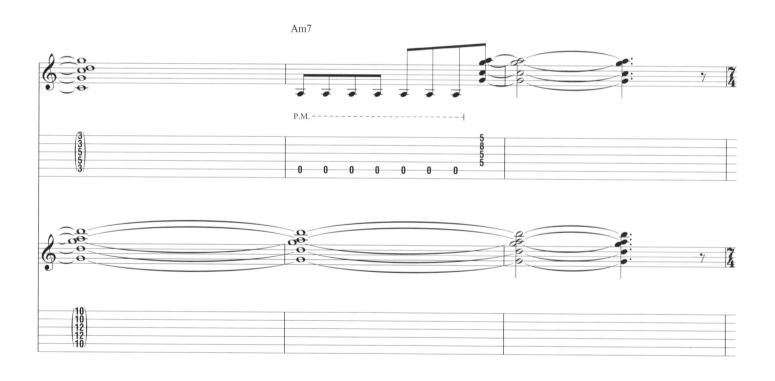

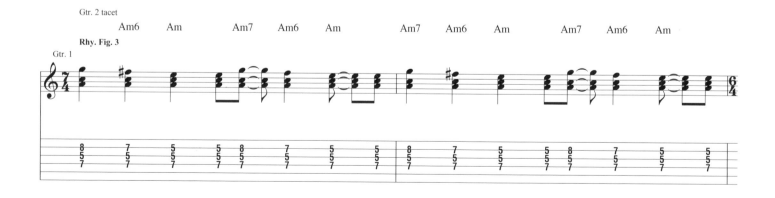

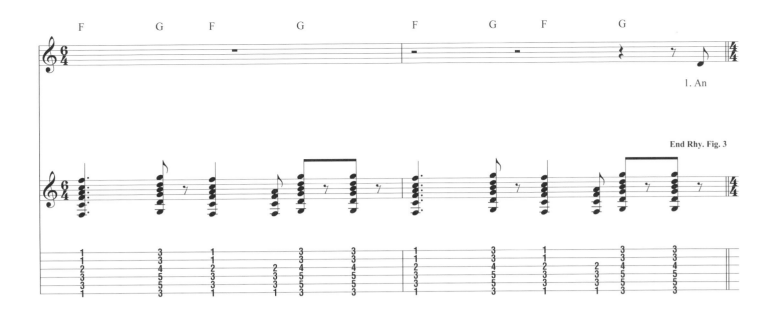

End Rhy. Fig. 3

Verse

Gtr. 1: w/ Rhy. Fig. 1
Gtr. 2: w/ Rhy. Fig. 2

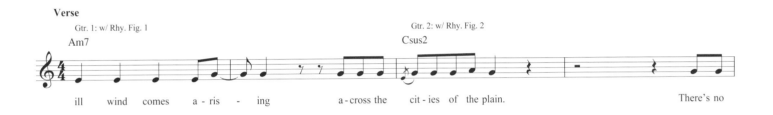

ill wind comes a - ris - ing a - cross the cit - ies of the plain. There's no

swim - ming in the heav - y wa - ter, no sing - ing in the ac - id rain. _____

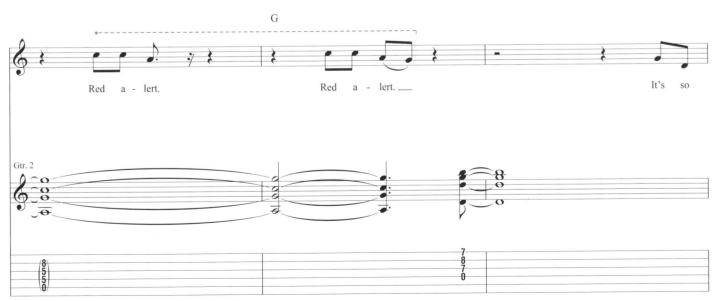

Red a - lert. Red a - lert. _____ It's so

*w/ delay set for half-note regeneration w/ 1 repeat.

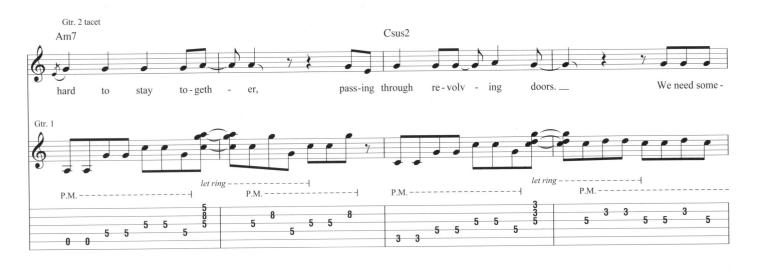

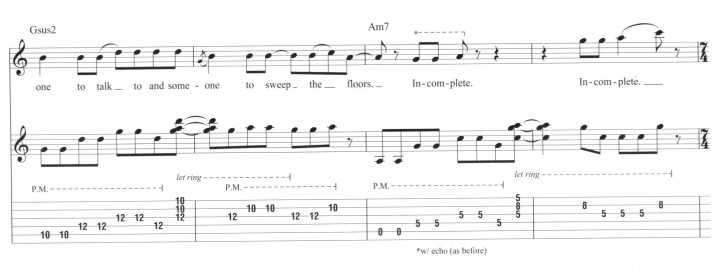

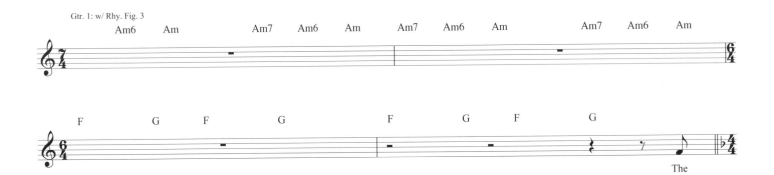

some - times drive me cra - zy, but I wor - ry a - bout __ you.

I

know it makes no dif - f'rence to what you're go - ing through, __

but I see __

To Coda 1

To Coda 2

__ the tip __ of the ice - berg and I wor - ry a - bout __ you.

let ring

delay & octaver off

Interlude

Gtr. 2: w/ Rhy. Fig. 2 (1st meas.)

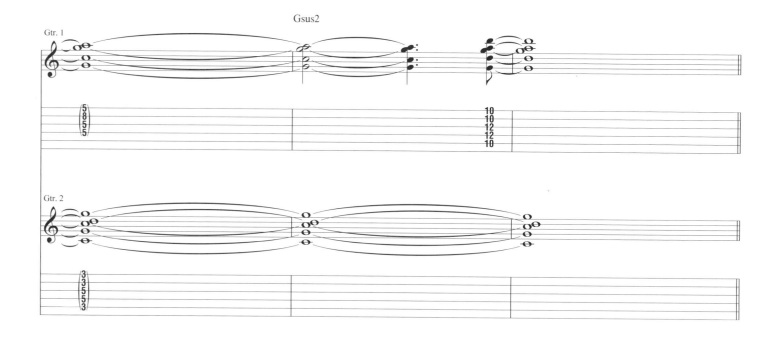

Verse

Gtr. 2 tacet

Am7   Asus4   Csus2

2. Cruis - ing un - der your ra - dar,   watch-ing from sat - el - lites.   Take a

G7sus⁴   Am7

page from the red book and keep them in your sights. __ Red a - lert.

*w/ delay (as before)

Asus4   G   Gsus4   G

Red a - lert.

let ring

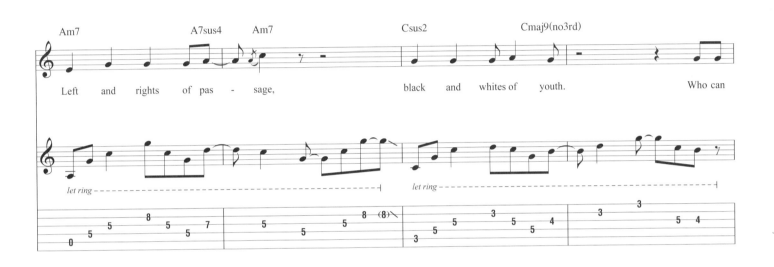

Am7   A7sus4   Am7   Csus2   Cmaj9(no3rd)

Left and rights of pas - sage,   black and whites of youth.   Who can

let ring

G7sus4   Am7   Am6   Am7

face the know - ledge that the truth is not the truth? Ob - so - lete.   Ab - so - lute, yeah.

let ring

*w/ delay (as before)

Interlude

Gtr. 1: w/ Rhy. Fig. 3

Am7   Am6   Am   Am7   Am6   Am   Am7   Am6   Am   Am7   Am6   Am

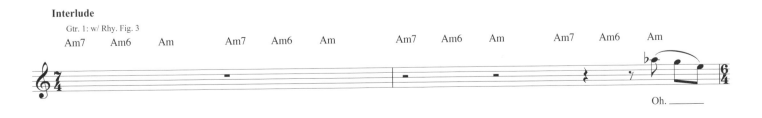

Oh. _____

The

Coda 1

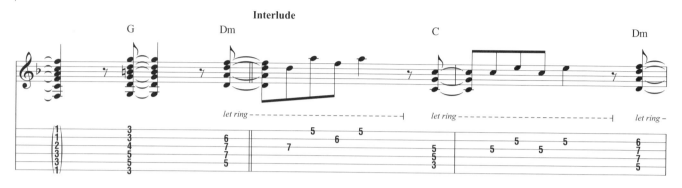

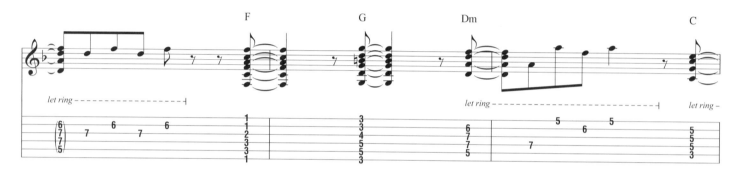

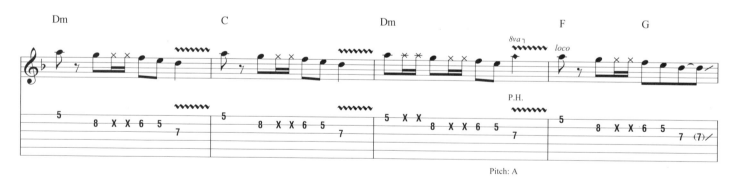

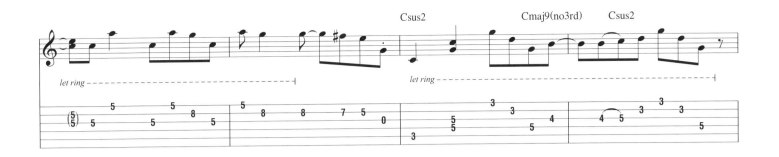

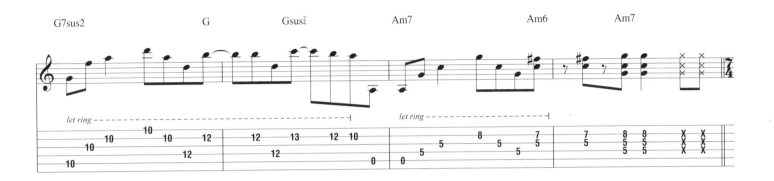

D.S. al Coda 2

The

Coda 2

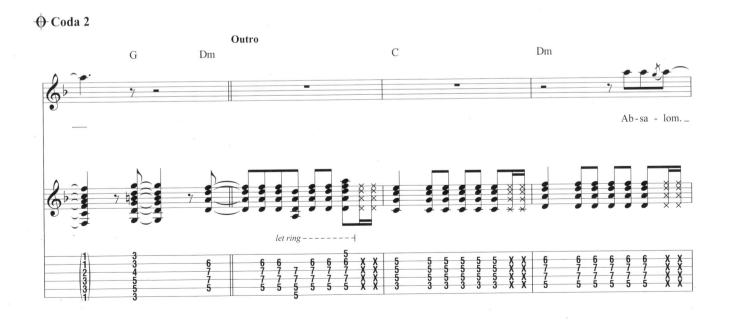

Ab - sa - lom.

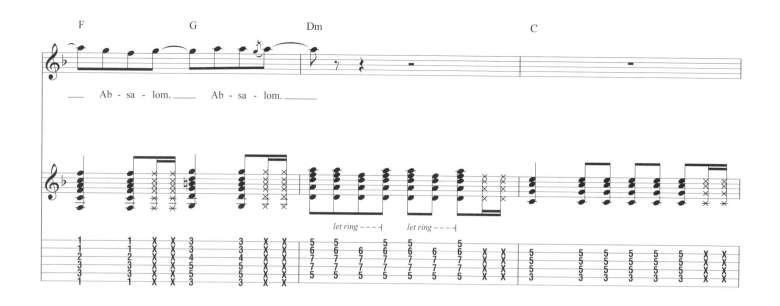

Ab - sa - lom. Ab - sa - lom.

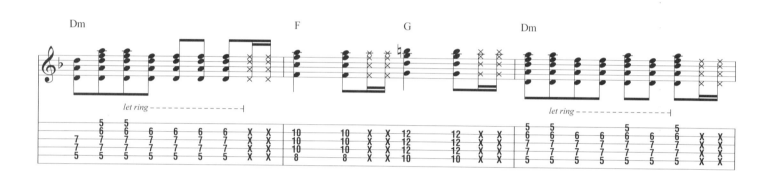

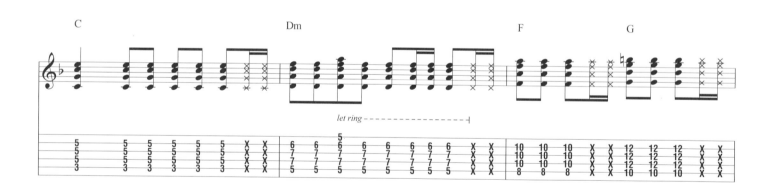

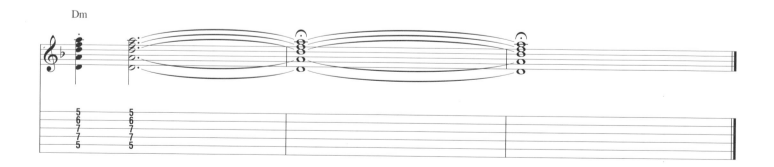

The Big Money

Words and Music by Alex Lifeson, Geddy Lee and Neil Peart

Tune up 1 step:
(low to high) F#-B-E-A-C#-F#

Intro
Moderately fast ♩ = 144

*Gtr. 1 (dist.)

*Three gtrs. arr. for one.

**Symbols in parentheses represent chord names
respective to up-tuned guitars. Symbols above
reflect actual sounding chords.

***Bass plays B.

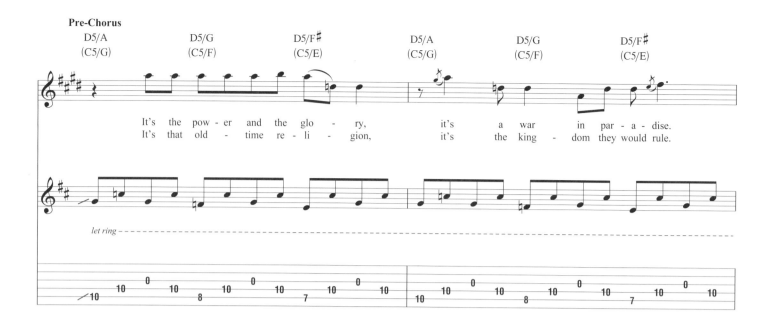

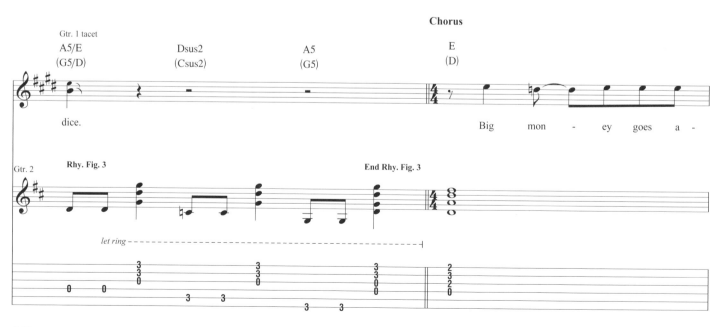

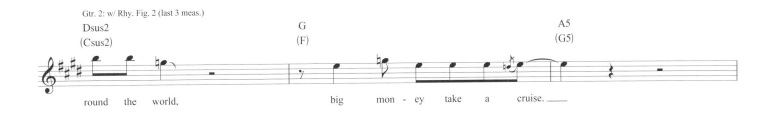

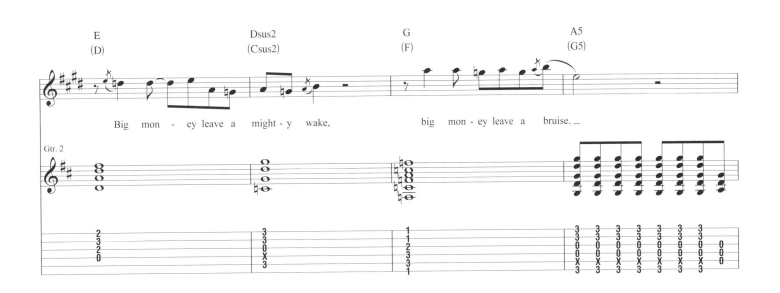

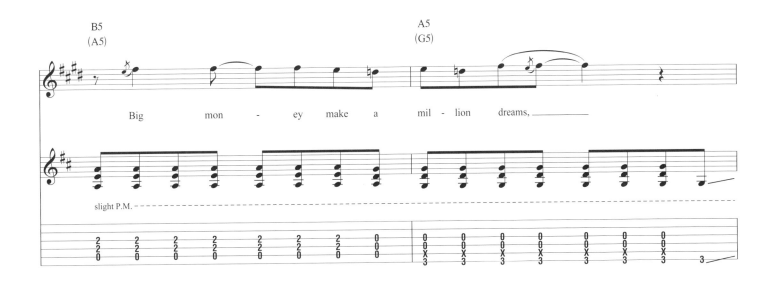

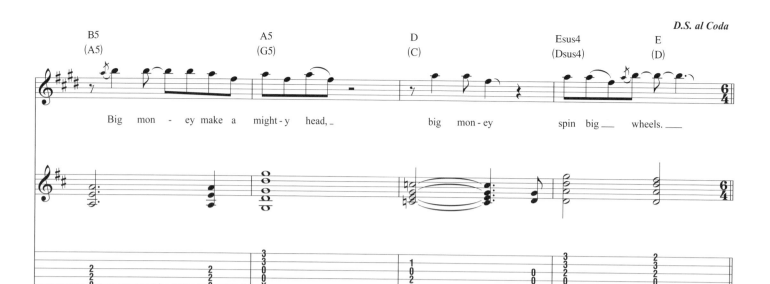

Big mon - ey make a might-y head, _ big mon - ey spin big _ wheels. _

Coda

Gtr. 1 tacet
Gtr. 2: w/ Rhy. Fig. 3 (4 times)

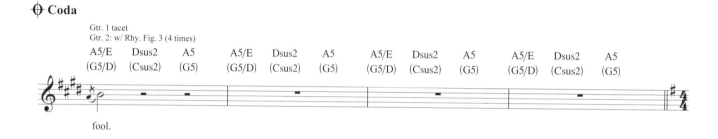

fool.

Interlude

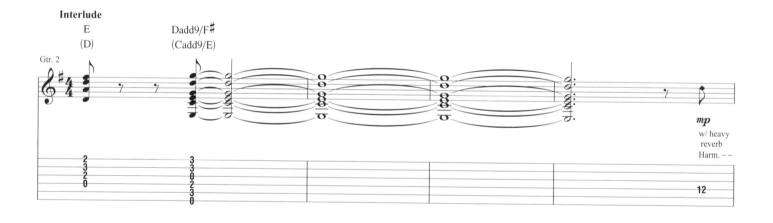

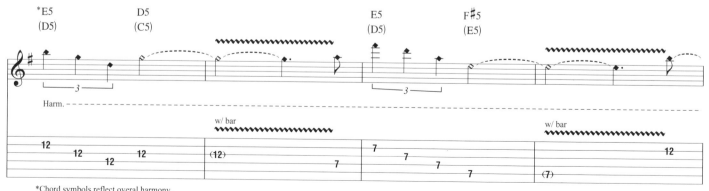

*Chord symbols reflect overal harmony.

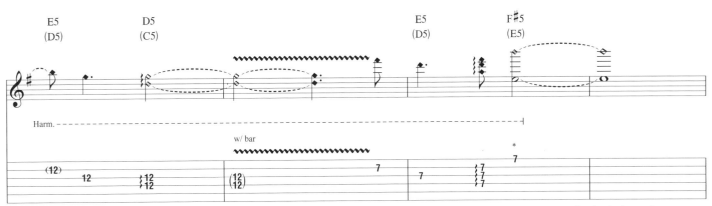

*Harm. & open string ring simultaneously.

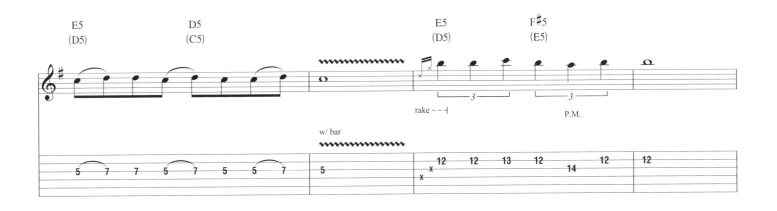

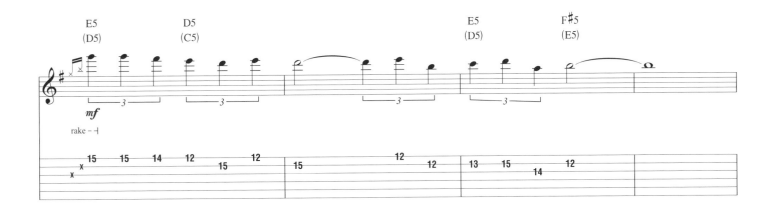

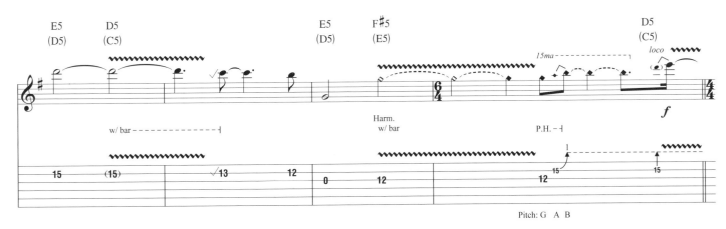

Pitch: G   A   B

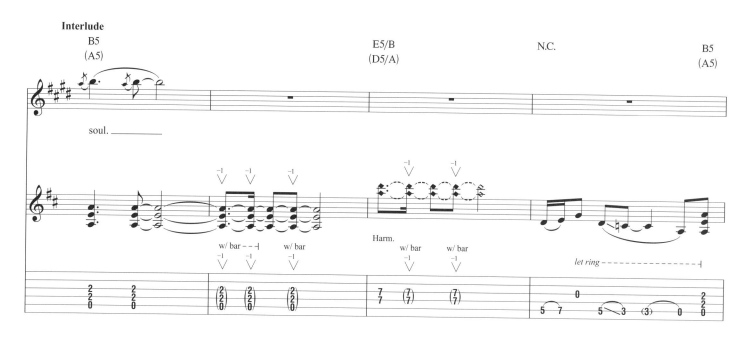

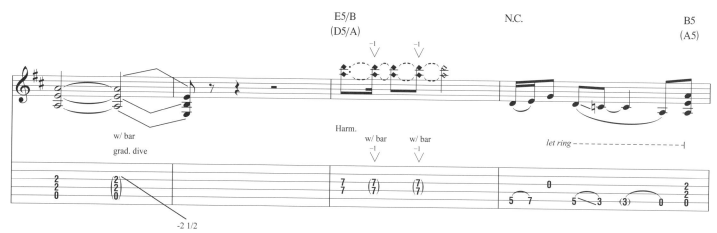

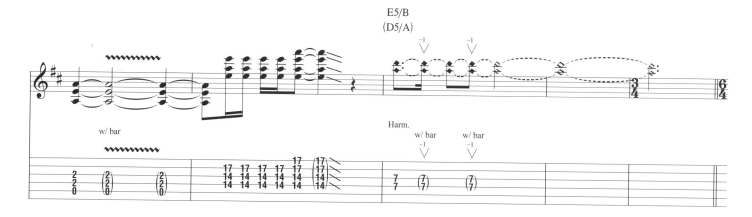

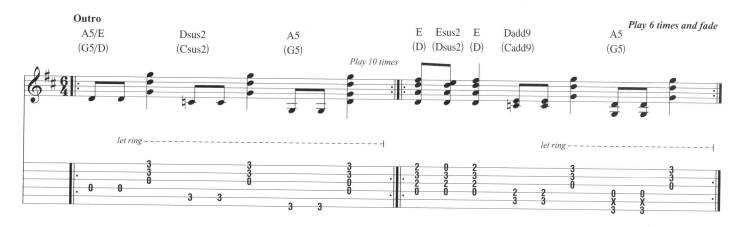

Force Ten

Words and Music by Alex Lifeson, Geddy Lee, Neil Peart and Pye Dubois

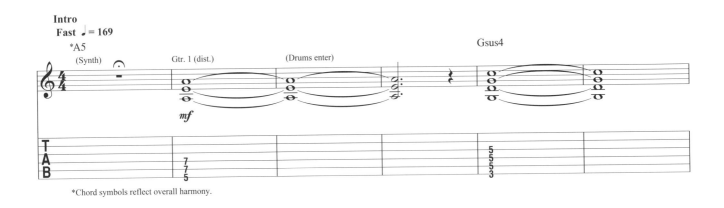

*Chord symbols reflect overall harmony.

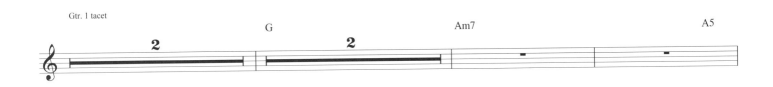

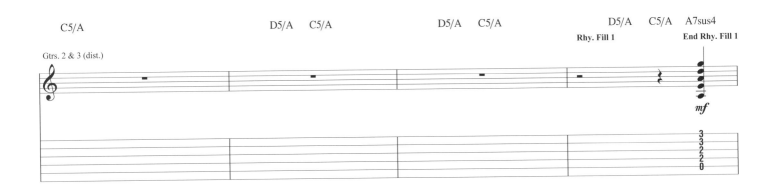

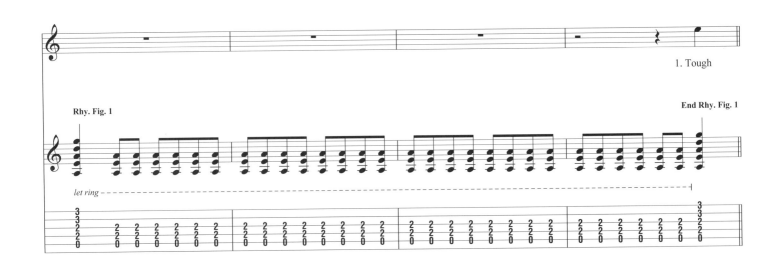

just — like pride. —

We can

Chorus

Gtrs. 2 & 3 tacet

*F♯5

D♯m

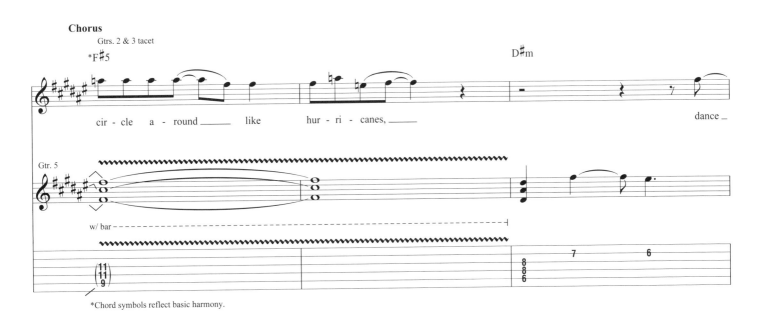

cir - cle a - round ___ like hur - ri - canes, ___

dance —

*Chord symbols reflect basic harmony.

C♯

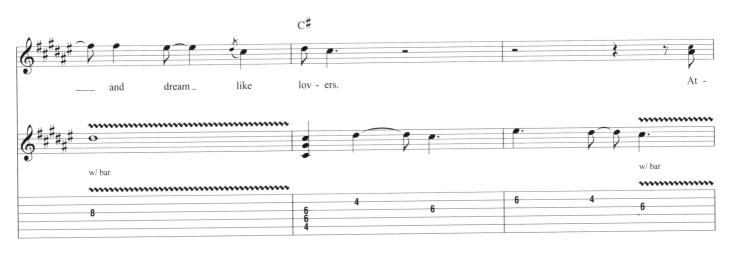

— and dream — like lov - ers.

At -

Gtrs. 2 & 3 tacet
*G

to the eye of the storm. Look out

Gtr. 6 Riff B
End Riff B

P.M.

Gtrs. 2 & 3

*Chord symbols reflect overall harmony.

Gtr. 6: w/ Riff B (2 times)
Am7
G

for the force with-out form. Look a-round

Fmaj7
G

at the sight and sound. Look in,

Am7
G
A7sus4

look out, look a-round.

Gtr. 6 Riff C
End Riff C

P.M.

Rhy. Fill 2
End Rhy. Fill 2

Gtrs. 2 & 3

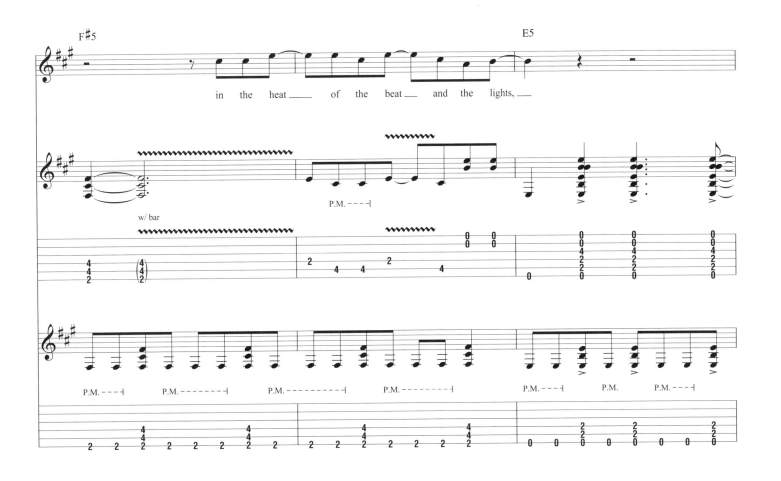

in the heat ___ of the beat ___ and the lights, ___

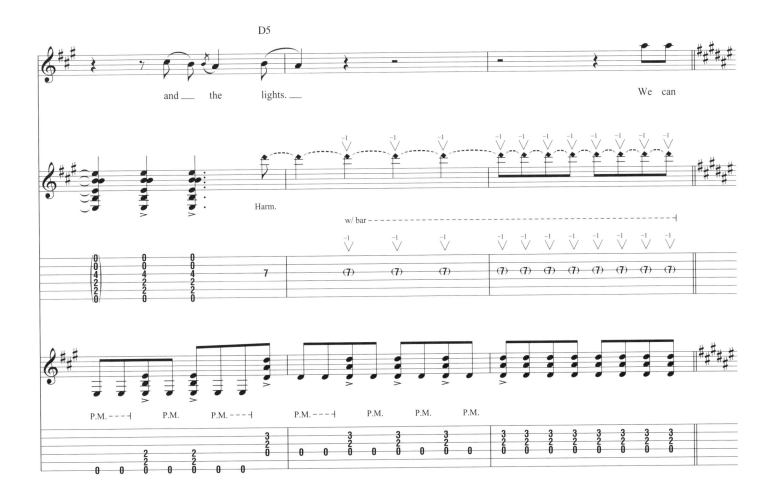

and ___ the lights. ___   We can

155

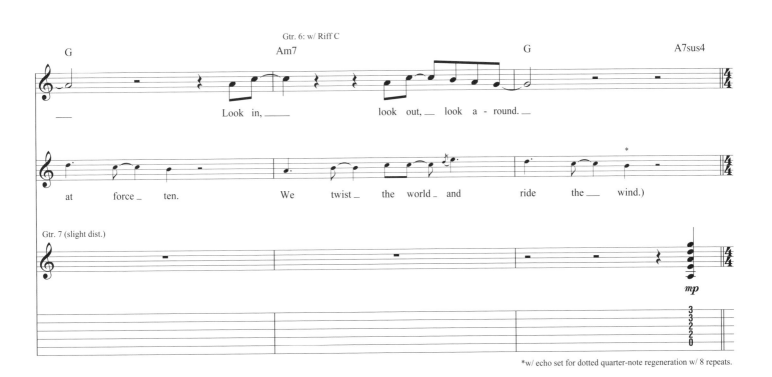

*w/ echo set for dotted quarter-note regeneration w/ 8 repeats.

Interlude

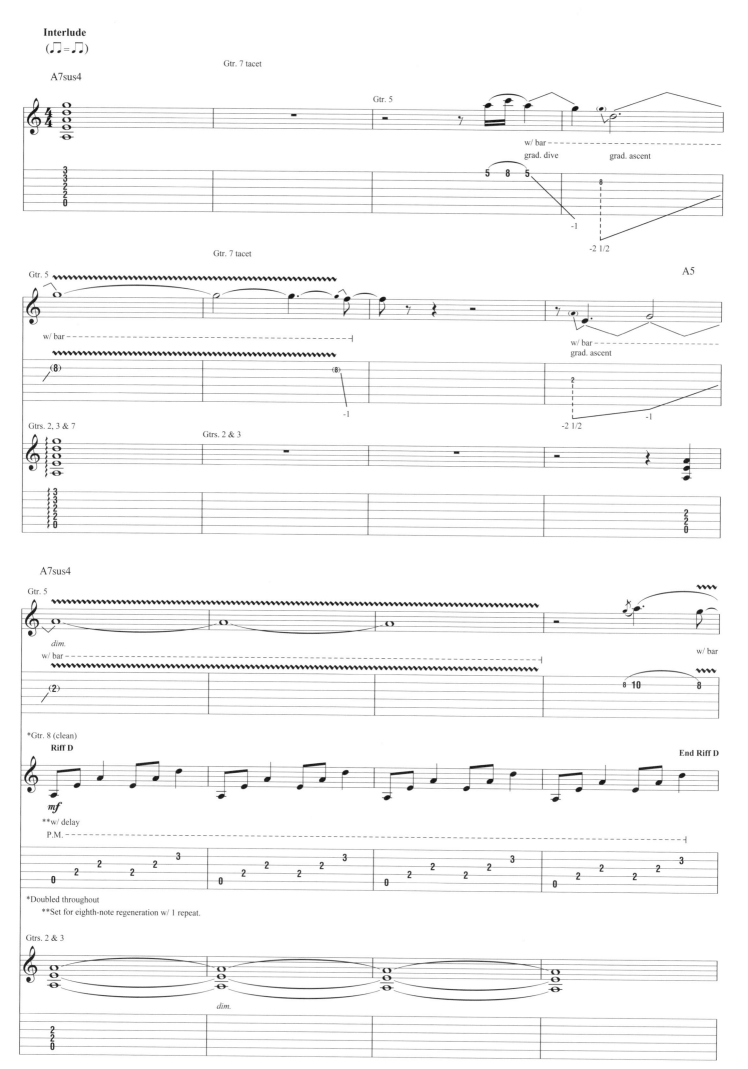

Gtrs. 2 & 3 tacet
Gtr. 8: w/ Riff D

Gtr. 5

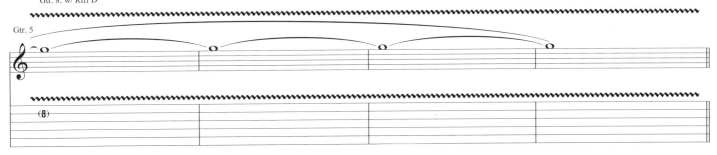

(8)

Interlude

Gtr. 5 tacet

*A7sus4   A7sus4/G   A7sus4   A7sus4/G

Gtr. 2

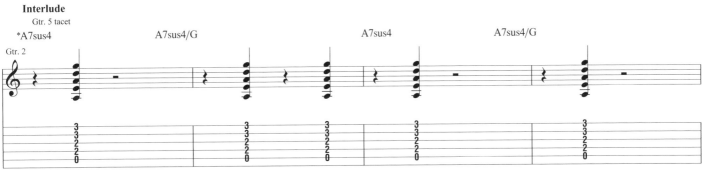

*Chord symbols reflect overall harmony.

A7sus4/F   A7sus4/G   A7sus4   A7sus4/G   A7sus4

3. Tough

Gtrs. 2 & 3

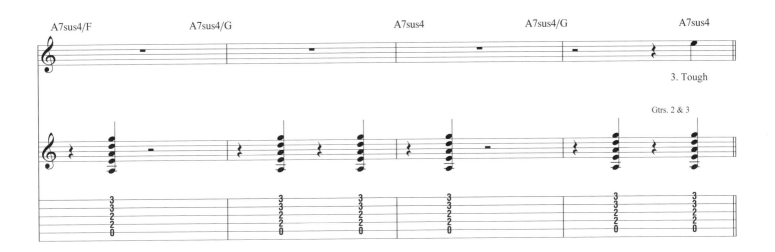

Verse

Gtr. 4: w/ Fill 1

A7sus4

times   de - mand ___ tough talk, de - mand ___ tough hearts, de - mand ___ tough songs. De - mand. ___

w/ bar

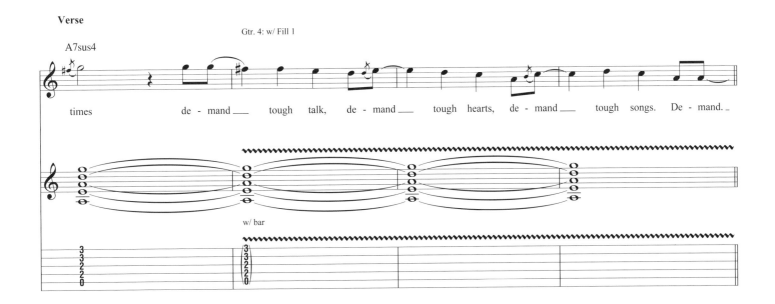

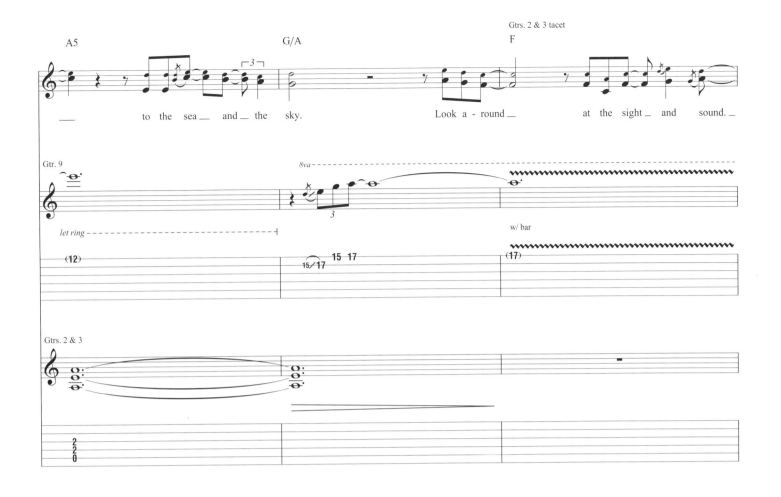

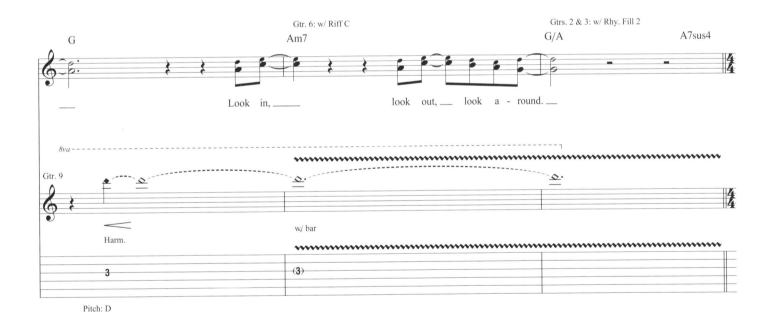

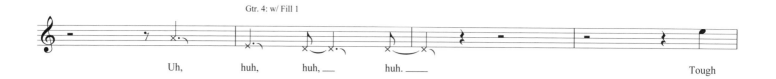

Gtr. 4: w/ Fill 1

Uh, huh, huh, ___ huh. ___ Tough

Gtrs. 2 & 3: w/ Rhy. Fig. 1

A7sus4

times de - mand ____ tough hearts.

Gtr. 4

w/ bar

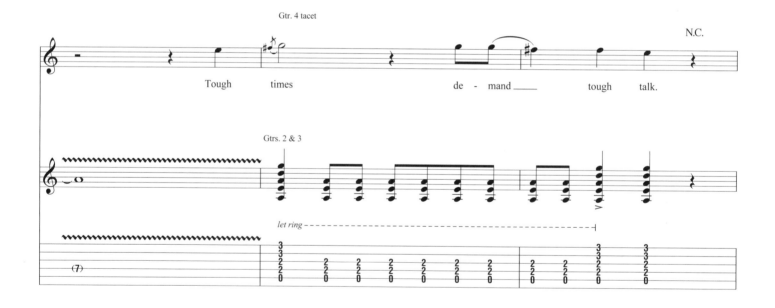

Gtr. 4 tacet

N.C.

Tough times de - mand ____ tough talk.

Gtrs. 2 & 3

let ring -

Gtrs. 2 & 3 tacet

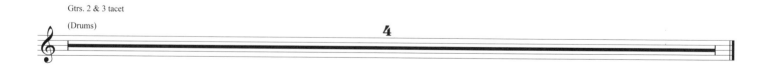

(Drums)

4

Time Stand Still

Words and Music by Alex Lifeson, Geddy Lee and Neil Peart

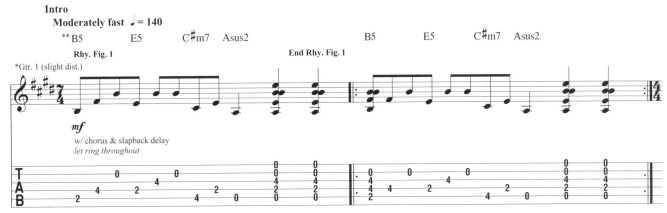

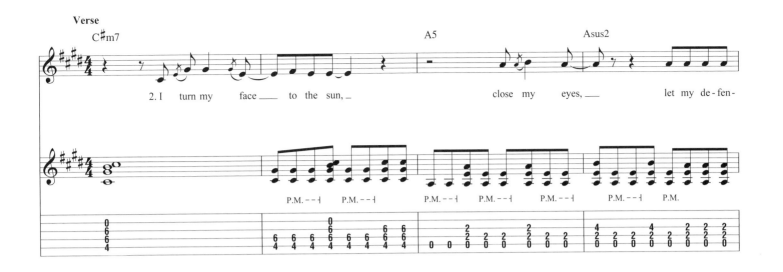

Aadd9   Badd11

I can wait un-til the tide comes a-round.

Pre-Chorus

Gtr. 2: w/ Riff A (2 times)

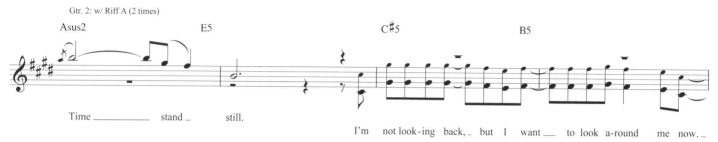

Asus2   E5   C#5   B5

Time   stand   still.

I'm not look-ing back, _ but I want _ to look a-round me now. _

Asus2   E5   C#5   B5

Time   stand _ still.

See more of the peo - ple and the

Gtr. 1: w/ Rhy. Fig. 1

E5   C#m7   Asus2

plac - es that sur - round me now.

𝄋 Chorus

Gtr. 1: w/ Rhy. Fig. 3

E5   Aadd9/C#   Badd11

Freeze this mo - ment a lit - tle bit long - er.
Sum-mer's go - ing fast, _ nights _ grow-ing cold - er.

Aadd9   F#m   E5

Make each _ sen - sa - tion a lit - tle bit strong - er.
Chil - dren grow-ing up, _ old friends _ grow-ing old - er.

Gtr. 1

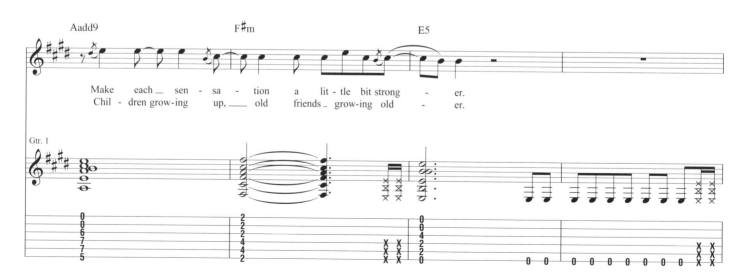

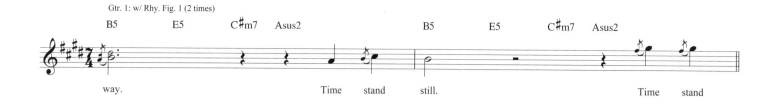

way.   Time stand still.   Time stand

still.

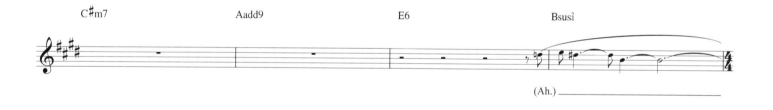

(Ah.)

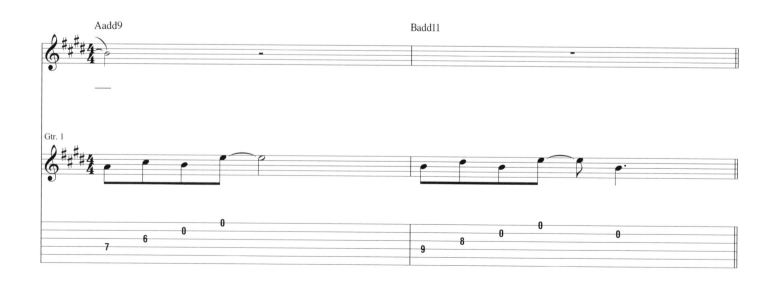

Pre-Chorus

Gtr. 2: w/ Riff A (2 times)

I'm not look-ing back, _ but I want _ to look a-round me now. _

_ See more of the peo - ple and the plac - es that sur-round me

Interlude

Gtr. 1: w/ Riff B

now. _____   Time stand still. ___

D.S. al Coda

⊕ Coda

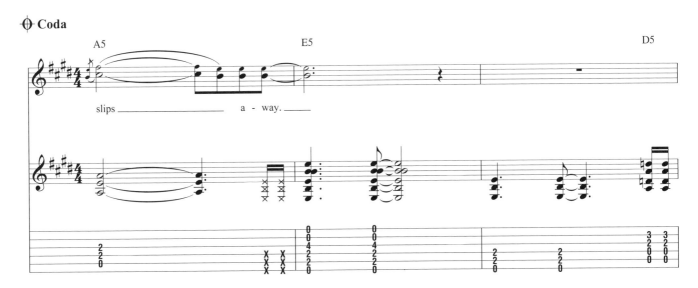

slips _____ a - way. ___

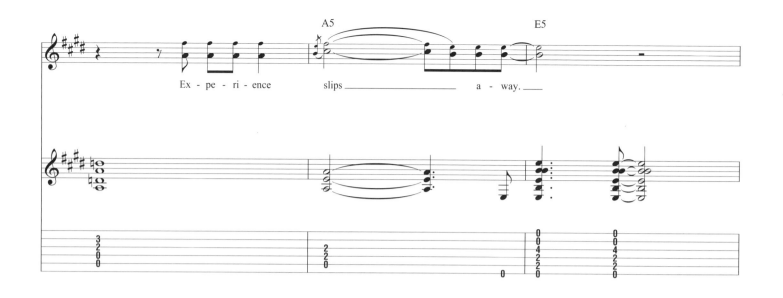

Ex - pe - ri - ence   slips _____ a - way. _____

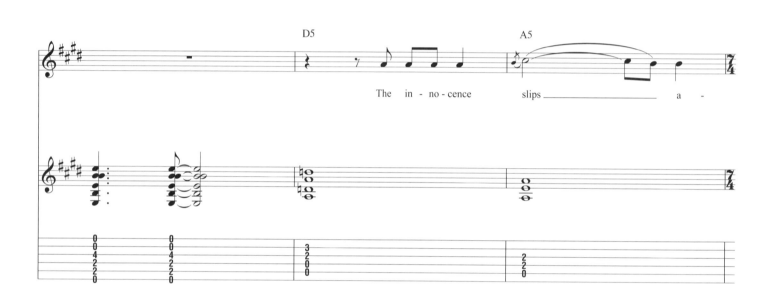

The in - no - cence   slips _____ a -

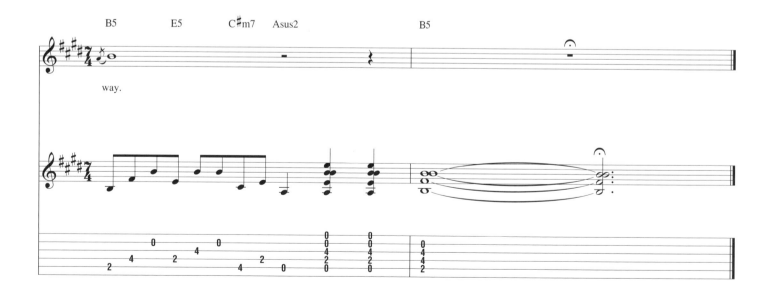

way.

GUITAR NOTATION LEGEND

Guitar music can be notated three different ways: on a *musical staff*, in *tablature*, and in *rhythm slashes*.

RHYTHM SLASHES are written above the staff. Strum chords in the rhythm indicated. Use the chord diagrams found at the top of the first page of the transcription for the appropriate chord voicings. Round noteheads indicate single notes.

THE MUSICAL STAFF shows pitches and rhythms and is divided by bar lines into measures. Pitches are named after the first seven letters of the alphabet.

TABLATURE graphically represents the guitar fingerboard. Each horizontal line represents a string, and each number represents a fret.

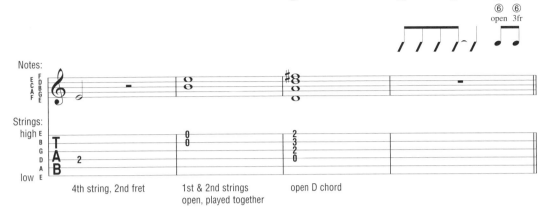

Definitions for Special Guitar Notation

HALF-STEP BEND: Strike the note and bend up 1/2 step.

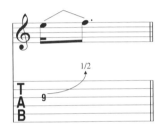

BEND AND RELEASE: Strike the note and bend up as indicated, then release back to the original note. Only the first note is struck.

VIBRATO: The string is vibrated by rapidly bending and releasing the note with the fretting hand.

LEGATO SLIDE: Strike the first note and then slide the same fret-hand finger up or down to the second note. The second note is not struck.

WHOLE-STEP BEND: Strike the note and bend up one step.

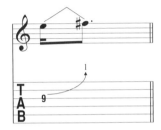

PRE-BEND: Bend the note as indicated, then strike it.

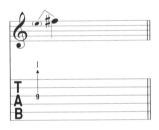

WIDE VIBRATO: The pitch is varied to a greater degree by vibrating with the fretting hand.

SHIFT SLIDE: Same as legato slide, except the second note is struck.

GRACE NOTE BEND: Strike the note and immediately bend up as indicated.

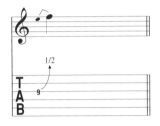

PRE-BEND AND RELEASE: Bend the note as indicated. Strike it and release the bend back to the original note.

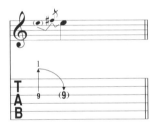

HAMMER-ON: Strike the first (lower) note with one finger, then sound the higher note (on the same string) with another finger by fretting it without picking.

TRILL: Very rapidly alternate between the notes indicated by continuously hammering on and pulling off.

SLIGHT (MICROTONE) BEND: Strike the note and bend up 1/4 step.

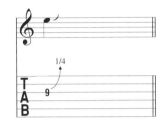

UNISON BEND: Strike the two notes simultaneously and bend the lower note up to the pitch of the higher.

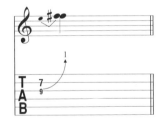

PULL-OFF: Place both fingers on the notes to be sounded. Strike the first note and without picking, pull the finger off to sound the second (lower) note.

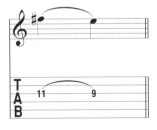

TAPPING: Hammer ("tap") the fret indicated with the pick-hand index or middle finger and pull off to the note fretted by the fret hand.

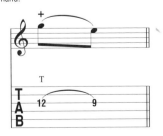

NATURAL HARMONIC: Strike the note while the fret-hand lightly touches the string directly over the fret indicated.

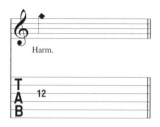

PINCH HARMONIC: The note is fretted normally and a harmonic is produced by adding the edge of the thumb or the tip of the index finger of the pick hand to the normal pick attack.

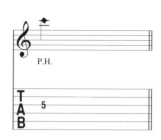

HARP HARMONIC: The note is fretted normally and a harmonic is produced by gently resting the pick hand's index finger directly above the indicated fret (in parentheses) while the pick hand's thumb or pick assists by plucking the appropriate string.

PICK SCRAPE: The edge of the pick is rubbed down (or up) the string, producing a scratchy sound.

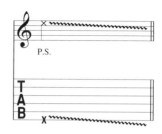

MUFFLED STRINGS: A percussive sound is produced by laying the fret hand across the string(s) without depressing, and striking them with the pick hand.

PALM MUTING: The note is partially muted by the pick hand lightly touching the string(s) just before the bridge.

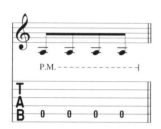

RAKE: Drag the pick across the strings indicated with a single motion.

TREMOLO PICKING: The note is picked as rapidly and continuously as possible.

ARPEGGIATE: Play the notes of the chord indicated by quickly rolling them from bottom to top.

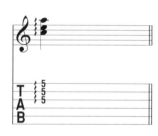

VIBRATO BAR DIVE AND RETURN: The pitch of the note or chord is dropped a specified number of steps (in rhythm), then returned to the original pitch.

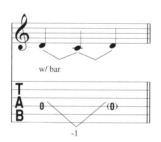

VIBRATO BAR SCOOP: Depress the bar just before striking the note, then quickly release the bar.

VIBRATO BAR DIP: Strike the note and then immediately drop a specified number of steps, then release back to the original pitch.

Additional Musical Definitions

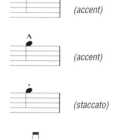

(accent)	• Accentuate note (play it louder).
(accent)	• Accentuate note with great intensity.
(staccato)	• Play the note short.
⊓	• Downstroke
V	• Upstroke

D.S. al Coda
• Go back to the sign (𝄋), then play until the measure marked "*To Coda*," then skip to the section labelled "**Coda**."

D.C. al Fine
• Go back to the beginning of the song and play until the measure marked "***Fine***" (end).

Rhy. Fig.
• Label used to recall a recurring accompaniment pattern (usually chordal).

Riff
• Label used to recall composed, melodic lines (usually single notes) which recur.

Fill
• Label used to identify a brief melodic figure which is to be inserted into the arrangement.

Rhy. Fill
• A chordal version of a Fill.

tacet
• Instrument is silent (drops out).

• Repeat measures between signs.

• When a repeated section has different endings, play the first ending only the first time and the second ending only the second time.

NOTE: Tablature numbers in parentheses mean:
1. The note is being sustained over a system (note in standard notation is tied), or
2. The note is sustained, but a new articulation (such as a hammer-on, pull-off, slide or vibrato) begins, or
3. The note is a barely audible "ghost" note (note in standard notation is also in parentheses).

GUITAR RECORDED VERSIONS®

Guitar Recorded Versions® are note-for-note transcriptions of guitar music taken directly off recordings. This series, one of the most popular in print today, features some of the greatest guitar players and groups from blues and rock to country and jazz.

Guitar Recorded Versions are transcribed by the best transcribers in the business. Every book contains notes and tablature unless otherwise marked. Visit **halleonard.com** for our complete selection.

The Beach Boys
00690503 Very Best $24.99
Beck
00690632 Beck – Sea Change ...$19.95
Jeff Beck
00691044 Best of Beck..............$24.99
00691042 Blow by Blow $22.99
00691041 Truth $19.99
00691043 Wired $19.99
George Benson
00694884 Best of......................$22.99
Chuck Berry
00692385 Chuck Berry..............$22.99
Billy Talent
00690835 Billy Talent $22.99
00690879 Billy Talent II............$19.99
Black Crowes
00147787 Best of $19.99
The Black Keys
00129737 Turn Blue $22.99
Black Sabbath
00690149 Black Sabbath $17.99
00690901 Best of......................$22.99
00691010 Heaven and Hell $22.99
00690148 Master of Reality $19.99
00690142 Paranoid $17.99
00690145 Vol. 4 ....$22.99
00692200 We Sold Our Soul
            for Rock 'n' Roll $22.99
blink-182
00690389 Enema of the State $19.95
00690831 Greatest Hits..............$24.99
00691179 Neighborhoods..........$22.99
Michael Bloomfield
00148544 Guitar Anthology $24.99
Blue Öyster Cult
00690028 Cult Classics $19.99
Bon Jovi
00691074 Greatest Hits..............$24.99
Joe Bonamassa
00158600 Blues of Desperation $22.99
00139086 Different Shades
            of Blue $22.99
00198117 Muddy Wolf at
            Red Rocks................$24.99
00283540 Redemption $24.99
Boston
00690913 Boston......................$19.99
00690932 Don't Look Back $19.99
00690829 Guitar Collection $24.99
David Bowie
00690491 Best of......................$19.99
Box Car Racer
00690583 Box Car Racer..........$19.95
Breaking Benjamin
00691023 Dear Agony $22.99
00690873 Phobia......................$19.99
Lenny Breau
00141446 Best of $19.99
Big Bill Broonzy
00286503 Guitar Collection $19.99
Roy Buchanan
00690168 Collection $24.99
Jeff Buckley
00690451 Collection..................$24.99
Bullet for My Valentine
00691047 Fever $22.99
00690957 Scream Aim Fire $22.99
00119629 Temper Temper $22.99
Kenny Burrell
00690678 Best of $22.99
Cage the Elephant
00691077 Thank You,
            Happy Birthday $22.99

The Cars
00691159 Complete Greatest Hits.$22.99
Carter Family
00690261 Collection..................$19.99
Johnny Cash
00691079 Best of......................$22.99
Cheap Trick
00690043 Best of......................$19.95
Chicago
00690171 Definitive
            Guitar Collection $24.99
Chimaira
00691011 Guitar Collection $24.99
Charlie Christian
00690567 Definitive Collection ..$22.99
Eric Church
00101916 Chief $22.99
The Civil Wars
00129545 The Civil Wars $19.99
Eric Clapton
00690590 Anthology..................$34.99
00692391 Best of......................$22.95
00694896 Blues Breakers
            (with John Mayall) $19.99
00138731 The Breeze $22.99
00691055 Clapton $22.99
00690936 Complete Clapton $29.99
00690010 From the Cradle $22.99
00192383 I Still Do $19.99
00690363 Just One Night $24.99
00694873 Timepieces................$19.95
00694869 Unplugged.................$24.99
00124873 Unplugged (Deluxe) ..$29.99
The Clash
00690162 Best of......................$19.99
Coheed & Cambria
00690828 IV $19.95
00139967 In Keeping Secrets of
            Silent Earth: 3 ....$24.99
Coldplay
00130786 Ghost Stories.............$19.99
00690593 A Rush of Blood
            to the Head $19.95
Collective Soul
00690855 Best of $19.95
Jessee Cook
00141704 Works Vol. 1 ....$19.99
Alice Cooper
00691091 Best of......................$24.99
Counting Crows
00694940 August &
            Everything After........$19.99
Robert Cray
00127184 Best of $19.99
Cream
00694840 Disraeli Gears $24.99
Creed
00288787 Greatest Hits..............$22.99
Creedence Clearwater Revival
00690819 Best of......................$24.99
Jim Croce
00690648 The Very Best $19.99
Steve Cropper
00690572 Soul Man...................$22.99
Crosby, Stills & Nash
00690613 Best of......................$29.99
Cry of Love
00691171 Brother $22.99
Dick Dale
00690637 Best of......................$19.99
Daughtry
00690892 Daughtry $19.95
Alex de Grassi
00690822 Best of......................$19.95

Death Cab for Cutie
00690967 Narrow Stairs $22.99
Deep Purple
00690289 Best of......................$22.99
00690288 Machine Head $19.99
Def Leppard
00690784 Best of......................$24.99
Derek and the Dominos
00694831 Layla & Other
            Assorted Love Songs..$24.99
Ani DiFranco
00690384 Best of......................$19.95
Dinosaur Jr.
00690979 Best of......................$22.99
The Doors
00690347 Anthology..................$22.95
00690348 Essential Collection ...$16.95
Dream Theater
00160579 The Astonishing $24.99
00122443 Dream Theater $24.99
00291164 Distance Over Time ..$24.99
Eagles
00278631 Their Greatest
            Hits 1971-1975 ....$22.99
00278632 Very Best of..............$34.99
Duane Eddy
00690250 Best of......................$19.99
Tommy Emmanuel
00147067 All I Want for
            Christmas $19.99
00690909 Best of $24.99
00172824 It's Never Too Late $22.99
00139220 Little by Little $24.99
Melissa Etheridge
00690555 Best of......................$19.95
Evanescence
00691186 Evanescence..............$22.99
Extreme
00690515 Pornograffitti.............$24.99
John Fahey
00150257 Guitar Anthology $19.99
Tal Farlow
00125661 Best of......................$19.99
Five Finger Death Punch
00691009 5 Finger Death Punch $19.99
00691181 American Capitalism..$22.99
00128917 Wrong Side of Heaven &
            Righteous Side of Hell.$22.99
Fleetwood Mac
00690664 Best of......................$24.99
Flyleaf
00690870 Flyleaf......................$19.95
Foghat
00690986 Best of......................$22.99
Foo Fighters
00691024 Greatest Hits..............$22.99
00691115 Wasting Light............$22.99
Peter Frampton
00690842 Best of......................$22.99
Robben Ford
00690805 Best of......................$24.99
00120220 Guitar Anthology $29.99
Free
00694920 Best of......................$19.99
Rory Gallagher
00295410 Blues (Selections).....$24.99
Danny Gatton
00694807 88 Elmira St..............$22.99
Genesis
00690438 Guitar Anthology $24.99
Godsmack
00120167 Godsmack..................$19.95
00691048 The Oracle $22.99
Goo Goo Dolls
00690943 Greatest Hits Vol. 1....$24.99

Grateful Dead
00139460 Guitar Anthology $29.99
Green Day
00212480 Revolution Radio $19.99
00118259 ¡Tré! $21.99
00113073 ¡Uno! $21.99
Peter Green
00691190 Best of $24.99
Greta Van Fleet
00287517 Anthem of the
            Peaceful Army..........$19.99
00287515 From the Fires..........$19.99
Patty Griffin
00690927 Children Running
            Through $19.95
Guns N' Roses
00690978 Chinese Democracy...$24.99
Buddy Guy
00691027 Anthology $24.99
00694854 Damn Right, I've
            Got the Blues............$19.95
Jim Hall
00690697 Best of......................$19.99
Ben Harper
00690840 Both Sides of the Gun .$19.95
00691018 Fight for Your Mind...$22.99
George Harrison
00694798 Anthology..................$22.99
Scott Henderson
00690841 Blues Guitar Collection$24.99
Jimi Hendrix
00692930 Are You Experienced?..$27.99
00692931 Axis: Bold As Love.....$24.99
00690304 Band of Gypsys..........$24.99
00690608 Blue Wild Angel.........$24.95
00275044 Both Sides of the Sky .$22.99
00692932 Electric Ladyland.......$27.99
00690017 Live at Woodstock $29.99
00119619 People, Hell & Angels $24.99
00690602 Smash Hits $24.99
00691152 West Coast Seattle
            Boy (Anthology)........$29.99
00691332 Winterland $22.99
H.I.M.
00690843 Dark Light................$19.95
Buddy Holly
00660029 Best of......................$22.99
John Lee Hooker
00690793 Anthology..................$29.99
Howlin' Wolf
00694905 Howlin' Wolf.............$22.99
Billy Idol
00690692 Very Best of..............$22.99
Imagine Dragons
00121961 Night Visions $22.99
Incubus
00690688 A Crow Left of the
            Murder......................$19.95
Iron Maiden
00690790 Anthology..................$24.99
00691058 The Final Frontier $22.99
00200446 Guitar Tab $29.99
00690887 A Matter of Life
            and Death $24.95
Alan Jackson
00690730 Guitar Collection $29.99
Elmore James
00696938 Master of the
            Electric Slide Guitar ..$19.99
Jane's Addiction
00690652 Best of......................$19.99
Jethro Tull
00690684 Aqualung..................$22.99
00690693 Guitar Anthology $24.99
00691182 Stand Up $22.99

John 5
00690898 The Devil Knows
My Name $22.95
00690814 Songs for Sanity.........$19.95
00690751 Vertigo $19.95

Eric Johnson
00694912 Ah Via Musicom $24.99
00690660 Best of......................$27.99
00691076 Up Close..................$22.99
00690169 Venus Isle.................$27.99

Jack Johnson
00690846 Curious George $19.95

Robert Johnson
00690271 New Transcriptions ...$24.99

Janis Joplin
00699131 Best of......................$19.95

Judas Priest
00690427 Best of......................$24.99

Kansas
00690277 Best of......................$19.99

Phil Keaggy
00690911 Best of......................$24.99

Toby Keith
00690727 Guitar Collection $19.99

The Killers
00690910 Sam's Town $19.95

Killswitch Engage
00120814 Disarm the Descent...$22.99

Albert King
00690504 Very Best of...............$24.99
00124869 In Session $22.99

B.B. King
00690492 Anthology..................$24.99
00130447 Live at the Regal $17.99
00690444 Riding with the King..$24.99

Freddie King
00690134 Collection $19.99

Marcus King
00327968 El Dorado $22.99

Kiss
00690157 Alive! $19.99
00690356 Alive II $22.99
00694903 Best of.......................$24.99
00690355 Destroyer $17.99
00291163 Very Best of $24.99

Mark Knopfler
00690164 Guitar Styles $24.99

Korn
00690780 Greatest Hits Vol. 1....$24.99

Kris Kristofferson
00690377 Collection..................$19.99

Lamb of God
00690834 Ashes of the Wake $24.99
00691187 Resolution $22.99
00690875 Sacrament $22.99

Ray LaMontagne
00690977 Gossip in the Grain ...$19.99
00691057 God Willin' & The
Creek Don't Rise $22.99
00690890 Til the Sun Turns Black$19.95

Jonny Lang
00690658 Long Time Coming $19.95

John Lennon
00690679 Guitar Collection $24.99

Linkin Park
00690922 Minutes to Midnight ..$19.99

Los Lonely Boys
00690743 Los Lonely Boys.........$19.95

The Lumineers
00114563 The Lumineers $22.99

George Lynch
00690525 Best of......................$24.99

Lynyrd Skynyrd
00690955 All-Time Greatest Hits. $24.99
00694954 New Best of $24.99

Yngwie Malmsteen
00690577 Anthology..................$29.99

Marilyn Manson
00690754 Lest We Forget...........$19.99

Bob Marley
00694956 Legend $19.99
00694945 Songs of Freedom $29.99

Maroon 5
00690657 Songs About Jane $19.95

Pat Martino
00139168 Guitar Anthology $24.99

John McLaughlin
00129105 Guitar Tab Anthology...$24.99

Mastodon
00690989 Crack the Skye $24.99
00236690 Emperor of Sand.......$22.99
00691176 The Hunter................$22.99
00137718 Once More 'Round
the Sun.....................$22.99

Andy McKee
00691942 Art of Motion $24.99
00691034 Joyland......................$19.99

Don McLean
00120080 Songbook..................$19.99

Megadeth
00690481 Capitol Punishment ...$22.99
00694952 Countdown to
Extinction...............$24.99
00691015 Endgame $24.99
00276065 Greatest Hits..............$24.99
00694951 Rust in Peace $24.99
00691185 Th1rt3en $22.99
00690011 Youthanasia $24.99

John Mellencamp
00690505 Guitar Collection $24.99

Metallica
00209876 Hardwired...
To Self-Destruct.........$22.99

Pat Metheny
00690562 Bright Size Life $24.99
00691073 Day Trip/
Tokyo Day Trip Live...$22.99
00690646 One Quiet Night........$24.99
00690559 Question & Answer....$24.99
00690565 Rejoicing...................$19.95
00690558 Trio 99-00.................$24.99
00690561 Trio Live...................$22.95
00118836 Unity Band $22.99
00102590 What's It All About....$24.99

Steve Miller Band
00690040 Young Hearts: Complete
Greatest Hits..............$24.99

Ministry
00119338 Guitar Tab Collection ..$24.99

Wes Montgomery
00102591 Guitar Anthology $24.99

Gary Moore
00691092 Best of.......................$24.99
00694802 Still Got the Blues......$24.99

Alanis Morissette
00355456 Jagged Little Pill $22.99

Motion City Soundtrack
00691005 Best of $19.99

Mountain
00694958 Best of $19.99

Mudvayne
00690794 Lost and Found $19.95

Mumford & Sons
00691070 Sigh No More $22.99

Muse
00118196 The 2nd Law $19.99
00151195 Drones......................$19.99

My Morning Jacket
00690996 Collection $19.99

Matt Nathanson
00690984 Some Mad Hope $22.99

Night Ranger
00690883 Best of $19.99

Nirvana
00690611 Nirvana.....................$22.95
00694895 Bleach......................$19.99
00694913 In Utero $19.99
00694883 Nevermind................$19.99
00690026 Unplugged in New York$19.99

No Doubt
00120112 Tragic Kingdom.........$22.95

Nothing More
00265439 Guitar & Bass Tab
Collection.................$24.99

The Offspring
00690807 Greatest Hits.............$22.99

Opeth
00243349 Best of $22.99

Roy Orbison
00691052 Black & White Night..$22.99

Ozzy Osbourne
00694847 Best of......................$24.99

Brad Paisley
00690933 Best of.......................$27.99
00690995 Play $24.99

Christopher Parkening
00690938 Duets & Concertos $24.99
00690939 Solo Pieces $19.99

Les Paul
00690594 Best of......................$22.99

Pearl Jam
00694855 Ten............................$22.99

Periphery
00146043 Guitar Tab Collection..$24.99

Carl Perkins
00690725 Best of $19.99

Tom Petty
00690499 Definitive Collection ..$22.99

Phish
00690176 Billy Breathes............$24.99

Pink Floyd
00121933 Acoustic Collection....$24.99
00690428 Dark Side of the Moon$19.99
00142677 The Endless River......$19.99
00244637 Guitar Anthology $24.99
00239799 The Wall...................$24.99

Poison
00690789 Best of......................$19.99

Elvis Presley
00692535 Elvis Presley $19.95
00690299 King of Rock 'n' Roll.$22.99

Prince
00690925 Very Best of...............$24.99

Queen
00690003 Classic Queen $24.99
00694975 Greatest Hits.............$25.99

Queens of the Stone Age
00254332 Villains $22.99

Queensryche
00690670 Very Best of...............$24.99

The Raconteurs
00690878 Broken Boy Soldiers ...$19.95

Radiohead
00109303 Guitar Anthology $24.99

Rage Against the Machine
00694910 Rage Against the
Machine...................$22.99
00119834 Guitar Anthology $24.99

Rancid
00690179 And Out Come the
Wolves.....................$24.99

Ratt
00690426 Best of......................$19.95

Red Hot Chili Peppers
00690055 BloodSugarSexMagik..$19.99
00690584 By the Way $24.99
00690379 Californication...........$19.99
00182634 The Getaway..............$24.99
00690673 Greatest Hits.............$22.99
00691166 I'm with You.............$22.99
00690255 Mother's Milk...........$19.95
00690090 One Hot Minute........$22.95
00690852 Stadium Arcadium.....$29.99

The Red Jumpsuit Apparatus
00690893 Don't You Fake It $19.99

Jerry Reed
00694892 Guitar Style of............$22.99

Django Reinhardt
00690511 Definitive Collection ..$24.99

Jimmie Rodgers
00690260 Guitar Collection $22.99

Rolling Stones
00690014 Exile on Main Street..$24.99
00690631 Guitar Anthology $29.99
00690186 Rock and Roll Circus . $19.95
00694976 Some Girls $22.95
00690264 Tattoo You $19.99

Angelo Romero
00690974 Bella..........................$19.99

David Lee Roth
00690685 Eat 'Em and Smile $22.99
00690694 Guitar Anthology $24.95
00690942 Songs of Van Halen ...$19.95

Rush
00323854 The Spirit of Radio $22.99

Santana
00173534 Guitar Anthology $27.99
00690031 Greatest Hits..............$19.95

Joe Satriani
00276350 What Happens Next ..$24.99

Michael Schenker
00690796 Very Best of...............$24.99

Matt Schofield
00128870 Guitar Tab Collection ..$22.99

Scorpions
00690566 Best of......................$24.99

Bob Seger
00690659 Greatest Hits Vol. 2....$17.95
00690604 Guitar Collection $22.99

Ed Sheeran
00234543 Divide......................$19.99
00138870 X $19.99

Kenny Wayne Shepherd
00690803 Best of......................$24.99
00151178 Ledbetter Heights $19.99

Shinedown
00692433 Amaryllis $22.99

Silverchair
00690196 Freak Show $19.95

Skillet
00122218 Rise..........................$22.99

Slash
00691114 Guitar Anthology $29.99

Slayer
00690872 Christ Illusion $19.95
00690813 Guitar Collection $19.99

Slipknot
00690419 Slipknot.....................$19.99
00690973 All Hope Is Gone $24.99

Smashing Pumpkins
00316982 Greatest Hits..............$22.99

Social Distortion
00690330 Live at the Roxy.........$22.99

Soundgarden
00690912 Guitar Anthology $24.99

Steely Dan
00120004 Best of......................$24.99

Steppenwolf
00694921 Best of......................$22.95

Mike Stern
00690655 Best of......................$24.99

Cat Stevens
14041588 Tea for the Tillerman..$19.99

Rod Stewart
00690949 Guitar Anthology $19.99

Stone Sour
00690877 Come What(ever) May $19.95

Styx
00690520 Guitar Collection $22.99

Sublime
00120081 Sublime....................$19.99
00120122 40 oz. to Freedom.....$22.99
00690992 Robbin' the Hood......$19.99

SUM 41
00690519 All Killer No Filler $19.95
00690929 Underclass Hero $19.95

Supertramp
00691072 Best of......................$24.99

Taylor Swift
00690994 Taylor Swift $22.99
00690993 Fearless....................$22.99
00115957 Red...........................$21.99
00691063 Speak Now $22.99

System of a Down
00690531 Toxicity.....................$19.99

James Taylor
00694824 Best of......................$19.99

Thin Lizzy
00694887 Best of......................$19.99

.38 Special
00690988 Guitar Anthology $22.99

Three Days Grace
00691039 Life Starts Now $22.99

Trans-Siberian Orchestra
00150209 Guitar Anthology $19.99

Merle Travis
00690233 Collection..................$22.99

Trivium
00253237 Guitar Tab Anthology...$24.99
00123862 Vengeance Falls.........$22.99

Robin Trower
00690683 Bridge of Sighs..........$19.99